JANE AUSTEN'S WORTHING

THE REAL SANDITON

ANTONY EDMONDS

AMBERLEY

We will venture to assert that there certainly is not a watering-place in the kingdom that can outvie Worthing, or excel it in its natural advantages.

John Mackoull, *A Sketch of Worthing* (1813)

The sea air and sea bathing together were nearly infallible, one or the other of them being a match for every disorder of the stomach, the lungs or the blood ... Nobody could catch cold by the sea; nobody wanted appetite by the sea; nobody wanted spirits; nobody wanted strength.

'Mr Parker', speaking in Jane Austen's *Sanditon* (1817)

Dedicated to John Mackoull and Edward Ogle,
the Cavalier and the Roundhead of early Worthing

First published 2013
This edition published 2015

Amberley Publishing
The Hill, Stroud
Gloucestershire, GL5 4EP

www.amberley-books.com

British Library Cataloguing in Publication Data.
A catalogue record for this book is available from the British Library.

ISBN 978 1 4456 5087 6 (paperback)
ISBN 978 1 4456 1983 5 (ebook)

Typeset in 9pt on 12pt Sabon.
Typesetting and Origination by Amberley Publishing.
Printed in the UK.

Contents

Jane Austen (1775–1817)
This familiar watercolour of Jane Austen, painted by her sister Cassandra about 1810, is the only portrait from life that is known to exist. Jane Austen's relations did not think it a particularly good likeness. (© National Portrait Gallery, London)

Introduction
Jane Austen and Early Worthing

The Real Sanditon

We know of only one visit to Worthing by Jane Austen. This was her stay of between seven and fifteen weeks in late 1805 with her mother, her sister Cassandra and her close friend Martha Lloyd, when she was twenty-nine and not yet a published novelist. However it is possible, for reasons that will be explained in a moment, that this was not Jane Austen's last visit to the town that provided the background to the novel she began writing in 1817, the year of her death.

Either way, it would be overly restrictive to confine this book to the Worthing of just a single year, and we have taken Jane Austen's Worthing as encompassing the first twenty-five years of the nineteenth century. This book is thus intended not just to be a snapshot of Worthing in 1805, but the portrait of an era. In addition, the story of Warwick House – Trafalgar House in *Sanditon* – is told in full, from its construction in about 1785 to its demolition in 1896.

Therefore, although the principal focus is on Jane Austen – and on the unfinished novel she set in a town that is Worthing in all but name – this book also paints a broad picture of Worthing as it was during the most interesting period in its history.

For 'the real Sanditon' is two things. First, it is the numerous features of early Worthing that make it a close match for Jane Austen's fictional town. Secondly, it is the actual town of Worthing, which was much more multi-faceted and socially diverse than the town in the novel.

In a letter of 16 December 1816 to her nephew James Edward Austen (known in the family as Edward), who had just completed his first term at Oxford, Jane Austen famously wrote: 'What should I do with your strong, manly, spirited Sketches, full of Variety & Glow? – How could I possibly join them on to the little bit (two Inches wide) of Ivory on which I work with so fine a Brush, as produces little effect after much labour?' The last twenty-four words are often quoted in isolation, giving the impression that Jane Austen accepted the view that her work was overly narrow. The context, however, shows that her comment was less than wholly serious – she was teasing Edward and light-heartedly playing with the idea of using some of his own prose in her novels. Nonetheless, there is more than a grain of truth in Jane Austen's remark, since there are many aspects of early nineteenth-century English life that are outside the reach of her novels. (Interestingly, however, A. C. Grayling writes in the introduction to his 2009 edition of *Sanditon*: 'I persist in thinking *Sanditon* would have turned out to be a larger piece of ivory than any yet inscribed by Austen.')

Either way, early Worthing was more varied than the quiet, sedate place that Jane Austen turned into Sanditon, or that Robert Bloomfield and Horace Smith evoked in their writings of about the same period (see Chapter 8); and it was populated not just by the rich and the well-born, people like *Sanditon*'s Mr Parker and Lady Dedham. It was also a boisterous, noisy, muddy little town, filled with all manner of human activity – a town that accommodated not only respectable citizens such as Edward Ogle and his fellow-members of the Board of Town Commissioners, but also louche, colourful and morally dubious figures such as John Mackoull and, briefly, Colonel Berkeley.

A further reason for extending our account of Worthing in the age of Jane Austen to the first twenty-five years of the nineteenth century is that the years 1801–25 were such an important – and indeed clearly defined – period in the history of the town. During the first dozen years of the century Worthing developed quickly under the leadership of Edward Ogle, at a time when the Napoleonic Wars imposed severe limitations on travel in Europe and English sea-side towns were flourishing. The next twelve years or so were a period of consolidation, with Worthing by now a well-organised resort and a destination for the rich and the titled.

Then, from about 1825, the town's fortunes declined as English holiday patterns changed, and in the 1830s – and again in the 1850s – there were periods of considerable economic distress. Worthing gradually lost its fashionable status, and came to be regarded as a quieter and more respectable alternative to Brighton, particularly suitable for children and invalids.[1]

The year 1825 is therefore the logical cut-off point for a book focusing on Worthing in the age of Jane Austen, even though by then Jane Austen herself had been dead for eight years.

The Edward Ogle Connection

As already indicated, we know of only one visit to Worthing by Jane Austen, but it is possible that there were others. One reason for suggesting this is the tone of the only reference to Edward Ogle in Jane Austen's correspondence. This comes in a letter written on 3 November 1813 from Godmersham Park, the home of her brother Edward, to her sister Cassandra, who is staying in London. Cassandra has clearly referred to Ogle in her most recent letter to Jane, prompting the following response:

> Sweet Mr Ogle. I dare say he sees all the Panoramas for nothing, has free-admittance everywhere; he is so delightful! – Now, you need not see anybody else.[2]

As we shall see in Chapter 2 of this book, Edward Ogle was a major figure in London's docklands, so the panoramas that Jane Austen is referring to were the splendid views of London from the river which Ogle was able to see 'for nothing' because he could travel up and down the Thames whenever he liked on the vessels that he and his brother owned. He therefore had 'free admittance' to London's finest scenery. In her final sentence Jane seems to be suggesting that friends of Ogle had no need to seek out commercial operators of boat trips, since Ogle would give them a tour of the Thames – and indeed that he was the perfect guide to the sights of the riverside.

This tantalisingly brief passage is suggestive in several respects. It is unlikely that 'sweet Mr Ogle' is an expression that Jane Austen would have used of someone she had known briefly eight years earlier and never been in contact with subsequently. The fact that Jane and Cassandra were still on relaxed terms with Ogle in 1813 suggests that the acquaintance that had developed in 1805 had grown into a friendship, and that there had been further meetings, whether in Worthing or elsewhere.

It is clear from what Jane writes that Cassandra is seeing Edward Ogle while she is in London, and Cassandra's easy access to him on this occasion confirms that the friendship had continued. Both Jane and Cassandra paid regular visits to London (either separately or together) and – while Ogle owned a large house in Worthing and was active in the management of the town – he also had important business interests in London and spent much of his time there.

However there is nothing implausible about a further visit (or visits) to Worthing by Jane and Cassandra. The Austens thought little of travel – the circumstances of their lives during most of the first decade of the nineteenth century made for a somewhat nomadic existence – and Worthing was fewer than fifty miles from Chawton, where Jane lived from July 1809 until two months before her death in July 1817. This was less than half the distance between Chawton and Godmersham Park, their brother Edward's house in Kent, which both sisters regularly visited. Thus it is entirely possible that Cassandra and Jane visited Worthing again after 1805. Indeed the fact that it was only in 1817 that Jane started writing the novel she set in a fictionalised Worthing suggests that her acquaintance with the town may recently have been refreshed, rather than that she was drawing only on memories of a dozen years before.

Indeed there is a firm piece of evidence that Worthing remained on the family map. This is that Cassandra returned to the town in October 1817, less than three months after her sister's death, with her eldest brother James, the rector of Steventon; his second wife Mary, Martha Lloyd's sister; and their son Edward, the nephew to whom Jane had written a year earlier about her little bit of ivory. The party stayed in lodgings at 10 South Street from 8 to 16 October.

All that we know about the visit is that Mary and Edward went to the theatre on 9 and 14 October, and that on 10 October Mary paid the washerwoman.[3] The main reason for the stay in Worthing was to provide James, who was very unwell – he died just over two years later – with a dose of healthy sea-air. On the face of it, it is a little surprising that Cassandra should have been a member of the party, or indeed that Worthing was the chosen resort, rather than one much nearer to Steventon such as Southsea or Bognor. Perhaps Worthing was chosen because Cassandra had spoken highly of the town that she and Jane had visited in 1805 (and possibly subsequently). Perhaps, indeed, Cassandra had arranged to call on 'sweet Mr Ogle' and tell him about the circumstances of her beloved sister's death – it is interesting that neither Cassandra nor her brother joined Mary and Edward at the theatre, so they must have had something else to do on those two evenings. Or perhaps Cassandra simply wanted to revisit a place which she had known in happier times and which, as Jane's confidante, she knew had been much on her sister's mind during the final year of her life, providing as it did the background for her last piece of fiction.

However, even if Jane Austen herself did return to Worthing, Sanditon needed for the purposes of her book to be a young resort that resembled the Worthing she had known in 1805 rather than the more fully developed town of a decade or so later; and certainly she does not introduce into her narrative any of the features of the mature town that she would have encountered on later visits, such as the theatre, which opened in 1807.

The Unfolding of the Evidence

It is only relatively recently that it has become known that Jane Austen had stayed in Worthing in 1805. There were a few references to a proposed stay in the town in two letters that she wrote in late August of that year to her sister Cassandra (see pages 32 and 35), but, since there was no confirmation that the visit actually took place, there was nothing for writers or researchers to follow up.

The necessary confirmation lay hidden in the diaries and letters of Jane Austen's niece Fanny Austen (later Knight), which are held at the Kent History and Library Centre in Maidstone. Deirdre Le Faye was the first to study these documents closely, and in 1989 she noted the essential facts about Jane Austen's stay in Worthing in the first edition of her book *Jane Austen: A Family Record*. Then in 2000, in *Fanny Knight's Diaries: Jane Austen Through Her Niece's Eyes*, Le Faye added the information – derived from the reference to 'Mr Stanfords' in Fanny's letter of 15 September 1805 to her former governess Miss Chapman – that the Austen party had stayed at, in Le Faye's words, 'Mr Stanford's house'. Five years later, Francis Short, who had been studying Fanny's letters and diaries during the course of his research into Jane Austen's links with Streatham, made the connection between 'Mr Stanfords' and Stanford's Cottage, still standing today in the heart of Worthing.

Short shared his discovery with the *Worthing Herald*, which on 15 September 2005 published a report by Ruth Barnett under the headline 'The day my Auntie Jane came to live in Worthing'. The paper also printed Short's transcriptions of the relevant diary extracts in full. (These also appear in Chapter 3 of this book. Fanny's handwriting in the diaries is often almost illegible, and close study of high-resolution scans of her original entries has enabled me to correct two or three errors made in the earlier transcriptions.)

My own interest in Worthing and its history began in 2009, after personal circumstances brought me into close contact with the town. At that time there was no reference to Jane Austen's

Letter from Fanny Austen to Miss Chapman, 15 September 1805
This section of the second page of the letter Fanny Austen wrote to her former governess two days before she set off for Worthing includes the important reference to 'Mr Stanfords, Worthing' which tells us where Jane Austen stayed in 1805. This address information had presumably reached Godmersham in a letter from Mrs Austen, who (with Martha Lloyd) had already been in Worthing for a number of weeks before the others set off for Sussex on 17 September.

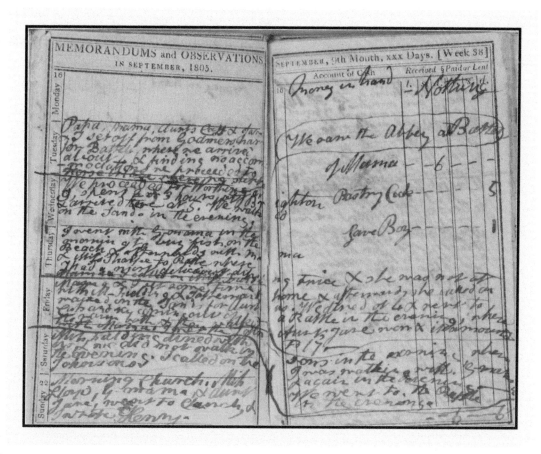

Fanny Austen's Diary Page for 16–22 September 1805

This is the diary page that includes Fanny's account of her week in Worthing. She and her parents left the town on 23 September. The barely legible scrawl in the diary entries contrasts with the neat handwriting Fanny used in the letter to Miss Chapman.

stay in any books about Worthing – it was not until October 2010 that, at the instigation of Janet Clarke, a blue plaque was fixed to the wall of Stanford's Cottage to commemorate the visit – and it was chance browsing on the internet that apprised me of the fact that Jane Austen had stayed in the town, and that it was believed that the fictional resort of Sanditon was based on Worthing.

I had never read *Sanditon*, but now did so, and quickly realised from my knowledge of Worthing's history and geography that the association with Worthing was much closer than had apparently so far been established. It was clear to me that the character of Mr Parker had been inspired by Edward Ogle; that Trafalgar House was based on Warwick House, where Edward Ogle lived; that Broadwater was the model for the village of 'old Sanditon'; and that Sanditon House had been suggested by aspects of Broadwater Manor and, in particular, Offington House.

There seemed to be potential for an article arising from these findings, but I then discovered that an article entitled 'Jane Austen and Worthing', by Janet Clarke, had been published in June

2009 in the *Jane Austen Society Report for 2008*. I made contact with the society and obtained a copy of the article. It was an interesting and evocative account of the Worthing that Jane Austen knew, but there was relatively little reference to *Sanditon* and no mention of Edward Ogle. No-one had yet made the connection between Mr Parker and Ogle, nor had Trafalgar House been identified with Warwick House, or the close links between the geography of Sanditon and Worthing been explored.

I therefore set to work on my own article, which was published in the *Jane Austen Society Report for 2010* in June 2011, under the title 'Edward Ogle of Worthing and Jane Austen's Sanditon'.

I had always hoped to expand my material into a book, and I am grateful to Nicola Gale, my editor at Amberley, for sharing my conviction that this was worth doing. The constraints of very tight relevance to Jane Austen meant that many fascinating aspects of Worthing in Jane Austen's era had had to be omitted from my article for the *Jane Austen Society Report*. Therefore – while much of the material from that article now appears in this book (albeit considerably reshaped) – much more is entirely new.

Although the arrangement of this book is primarily thematic, the sequence is also almost entirely chronological: Warwick House arrived in Worthing before Edward Ogle, and Jane Austen after both; John Mackoull followed. The 'notable visitors' of the final chapter, however, appear within their own separate time-sequence, from 1805 to 1825.

The Title of 'The Last Work'

Jane Austen began writing the novel that is today known as *Sanditon* in January 1817, and abandoned it in the middle of March when she became too ill to continue. In spite of the fact that during its composition she was suffering from the painful and debilitating illness that killed her, there is little evidence of any diminution in her powers, and had the book been finished it is likely that it would have been the equal of her six famous completed novels.

We do not know what Jane Austen herself intended to call the book, since her manuscript had no title. It is widely held among Austenians that her own title would have been *The Brothers* – which would have been appropriate to the theme and subject matter – but there is only one source for this information, Edward Thomas Austen, fifth son of Jane's brother Frank, who communicated it to his daughter, Janet Sanders, in a letter of 8 February 1925.[4]

When another of Jane Austen's nephews, James Edward Austen-Leigh, included lengthy extracts from the book in the second edition (1871) of his *A Memoir of Jane Austen*, he refers to it simply as *The Last Work*. The full text of the incomplete novel was first published in 1925 under the title *Fragment of a Novel*. Subsequent versions, however, have always been known as *Sanditon* – which seems also to have been the book's unofficial title among members of the Austen family from about the middle of the nineteenth century.[5]

Quotations

The quotations from *Sanditon* are taken from the 1975 edition of *Minor Works*, edited by R. W. Chapman, which was first published by the Oxford University Press in 1954. This definitive edition of Jane Austen's text is faithful to her original manuscript and includes its flaws and idiosyncrasies. It is both fascinating and instructive to read Jane Austen's prose in the vigorous but slightly chaotic form in which she originally set it down.

Wherever possible, quotations from other old texts are also given in the form in which they first appeared, reproducing, for example, the italics that were often scattered around early books and the over-generous use of commas that was characteristic of the period.

Money

In a number of places in the text sums of money are mentioned. It is never easy to determine what these long-ago sums of money represent in modern terms. The most direct comparison is to use Retail Price Index (RPI) figures, which tell us the amount of money that a given item would cost today. However a more meaningful result may often be achieved from a calculation based on the average earnings (AE) in the two years being compared.[6]

The two methods produce dramatically different figures. We will take the years 1810 and 2010 as our standard axes of comparison. In 1810 the British currency was not decimal: there were twelve pence in a shilling, and twenty shillings in a pound. According to the Measuring Worth website, a penny in 1810 was worth £0·23 (RPI) or £3·08 (AE) in 2010 values. A shilling was worth £2·77 (RPI) or £37 (AE). A pound was worth £55 (RPI) or £740 (AE).

The website provides figures for every historical year – although the modern axis is always 2010 – and we give three sample calculations here. Jane Austen's raffle winnings of seventeen shillings on 19 September 1805 amounted to either £54 (RPI) or £699 (AE). A figure towards the lower end of this range probably makes best sense. Edward Ogle's purchase of the Warwick House estate for £5,000 in 1801 represents either £297,000 or £4,820,000. Here the sum that floats into one's head is about half-way between these two figures. We do not know in what year John Luther paid a fellow-gambler £50,000 after he lost a wager, but if we take it to be 1785 – the approximate year that he built Warwick House – we get figures of £4,940,000 or £67,000,000. He must have been a rich man.

Illustrations

The picture on the front cover is a view of South Street looking towards the sea. The New Inn and the Sea House Inn are either side of the sea-end of the street, and the Nelson Inn is the building at centre-left with the porch and the overhanging sign. The engraving must date from about 1825, since George Cortis's butcher's shop, seen on the right of the Nelson Inn, opened in 1823, and the old Sea House Inn was rebuilt in 1826. The picture on the back cover, which depicts Montague Terrace, the Sea House Inn and the New Inn, is a watercolour of *c.* 1805–10 by John Nixon.

The illustrations on the front and back cover and on pages 15 (bottom), 33 (bottom), 43 (both), 53 (bottom), 54 (bottom), 57 (top), 77 (top), 78 (bottom), 88 and 89 (both) are reproduced by courtesy of Worthing Museum and Art Gallery; those on pages 33 (top), 37 (bottom), 44 (both), 54 (top) and 66 (bottom) by courtesy of West Sussex County Council Library Service, www. westsussexpast.org.uk; those on pages 4, 84, 96 (both), 102, 105, 117 and 118 by courtesy of the National Portrait Gallery; and those on pages 113 and 114 by courtesy of the British Museum.

The extracts from Fanny Austen's letter and diary on pages 8 and 9 are reproduced by courtesy of Kent County Council Kent History and Library Centre; Mr Ogle's Plan on page 24 by courtesy of the National Maritime Museum, London; the watercolour of Fanny Austen on page 34 by courtesy of the Jane Austen Memorial Trust; the engraving of the Theatre Royal and Warwick House on page 73 by courtesy of Robert Elleray; and the picture of the George Inn, Hayes on page 83 by courtesy of Bromley Library.

Most of the other illustrations come from the series of books about Worthing's history published under the Worthing Art Development Scheme between 1938 and 1955. All but the first of these were published by Aldridge Bros of 35 Warwick Street, Worthing.

Acknowledgements

The author would like to thank the following for their help in providing him with illustrations for this book: Emma Butterfield, Senior Rights and Images Officer, National Portrait Gallery; Julie Cochrane, Picture Librarian, National Maritime Museum; Martin Hayes, County Local Studies Librarian, and Emma White, Heritage Project Manager, both of West Sussex County Council Library Service; Arthur Holden of the Local Studies and Archives Department, Bromley Library; Hamish MacGillivray and Emma Walder, Arts and Exhibitions Curators at Worthing Museum and Art Gallery, and their photographical and curatorial volunteers; and Chris Sutherns, Editorial Account Manager, British Museum Images.

The author is also grateful to the late David Selwyn for publishing the article that forms the nucleus of this book in the *Jane Austen Society Report for 2010*; to Shane Hudson for doing the graphic design for the original version of the (now slightly amended) conjectural plan of Worthing in 1805; to Dr Helen Wicker of the Kent History and Library Centre, Maidstone for providing scans and photocopies of Fanny Austen's diaries and letters; and to Joanna Nortcliff for moral and practical support.

The Author

Antony Edmonds was born in Southsea and educated at Churcher's College, Petersfield and Magdalen College, Oxford. His other books are *Oscar Wilde's Scandalous Summer: The 1894 Worthing Holiday and the Aftermath* (2014), a detailed account of the eight-week period during which Wilde wrote *The Importance of Being Earnest*; and *Worthing: The Postcard Collection* (2013), a selection of 163 Edwardian postcards of Worthing, with historical commentary. He lives in a village on the Hampshire / Sussex border.

Chapter 1

Warwick House – The Model for 'Trafalgar House'

Warwick House was the most important house in the history of Worthing, and its construction in the late eighteenth century was the single event that more than any other set in motion Worthing's transition from fishing and farming village to fully fledged seaside resort. Then, through most of the eleven decades that Warwick House stood at the heart of Worthing, its fortunes ran parallel to those of the town.

Since it was on Warwick House that Jane Austen based Trafalgar House, which features prominently in *Sanditon*, it is of interest to tell the story not just of its early years, but also of its chequered and often rather sad existence over the eighty years after Jane Austen's death.[1] The evidence from the text of *Sanditon* that Trafalgar House was modelled on Warwick House will, like the other links between Worthing and Sanditon, be explored in Chapter 5.

But before we embark upon the story of Warwick House, we must briefly set it in its historical and geographical context.

At the start of the eighteenth century, what is now the borough of Worthing was a collection of separate settlements, including Broadwater, Tarring, Goring, Heene and Worthing. Worthing was the least important of these. Too small even to have a church, it 'consisted only of the mean abodes of needy fishermen, and of those persons who afforded assistance to the numerous smugglers, which at that time haunted all the southern coast in the character of a numerous banditti'. Smuggling gradually decreased as roads to the coast improved, allowing fishing to become a profitable business. Then, around the middle of the eighteenth century – when the benefits of salt water and sea air began to be promoted by the medical profession – 'some infirm and sickly strangers surprised the village with their first visits'.[2]

If we are to believe the evidence of one visitor of the time, early Worthing seems not to have been welcoming to these strangers. This unnamed visitor, who published a fifty-line poem in the *Lady's Magazine* in 1789, stayed partly in Worthing and partly in 'hospitable Tarring', where he finds his hosts generous and friendly. When his visit to the area ends, he is delighted to say farewell to Worthing's 'inhospitable shores', which he is leaving to go to 'climes far off' where he hopes to meet 'inhabitants more gentle'. He says that if it were not for the 'even sands and placid waves' that attract visitors, the name of Worthing would soon be 'confin'd to dark oblivion', since its people are 'of manners rough, and language most uncouth'; and the prices they charge are exorbitant. Only his acquaintance with a charming young woman he names only as B—s, who accompanied him on his walks, prevented him from being 'most uncomfortable and forlorn' during his stay in Worthing. He ends by making it clear that if he ever travels that way again, he will go straight to Tarring and avoid Worthing altogether.[3]

Until towards the end of the eighteenth century, the inhospitable village of Worthing remained the isolated agricultural and fishing community it had been for centuries. Its farms and homesteads, fields, gardens and orchards were dotted either side of the southern section of the long road that wound towards the sea from Broadwater. This southern section was called Worthing Street, and some of the land either side of it was later to become the Warwick House estate.

Worthing Street divided into two at what is today the junction of High Street and Brighton Road, at the north-west corner of Steyne Gardens. One branch, known as West Lane, followed the line of present-day Warwick Street and South Street and ended on the seafront opposite where the pier now stands. The other branch, East Lane, ran only a couple of hundred yards, as far as modern-day St George's Road, before turning sharply south towards the sea.

In earlier times there had been a coastal road between Worthing and South Lancing, but this had long since been washed away as the coastline advanced, so all traffic between Chichester and Brighton by-passed the town. In 1807, however, the town commissioners decided that a new road 'from the corner of Mr Ogle's wall in East Lane' to Lancing should be built at the commissioners' expense, and the road was completed towards the end of 1808. (Worthing remained under the parish of Broadwater until 1803, but in that year the Worthing Town Act was passed, setting up a Board of Town Commissioners with powers to levy rates and to maintain and police the town.)

At the end of the seventeenth century the land on which Warwick House was in due course built was owned by William Wade, the rector of Broadwater. In 1702 Wade sold the land to John Booker of Arundel, and it was then inherited first by Booker's widow and then by his grand-daughter. Finally, in 1780, the land was sold to John Luther, the MP for Essex, who already had an estate at Petworth. Luther supposedly – but probably apocryphally – once lost £100,000 on a single throw of the dice, but paid only £50,000. Even this lesser amount was a vast sum of money, and Luther's loss was regarded as 'a dear tax on dissipation and folly'.[4]

It was Luther that built a handsome house on this land. The date of its construction is not known. However it does not appear on a map of Worthing of 1778–83[5] and it was certainly in place by 1789, so it must have been built in the mid to late 1780s.

The house occupied a site north of the junction of modern-day High Street and Brighton Road and just south of where 12–16 Elm Road stand today. Its front façade was parallel with the end of Ann Street, and the central section was opposite the east side of Steyne Gardens. The house, which was built of flint with yellow brick dressings, initially had no name, being described simply as a 'marine residence'.

Luther died in 1786, and in 1789 the estate was sold to George Greville, 2nd Earl of Warwick (1746–1816). The house, which the earl enlarged in 1790, then became known as Warwick House. His primary residence, however, remained Warwick Castle, 140 miles away, and his association with Worthing turned out to be brief. In the aftermath of the French Revolution of 1789, Britain was at war with France, and in 1795 the earl became a colonel in the Warwickshire Fencibles, a kind of early version of the Home Guard, and was appointed Lord Lieutenant of Warwickshire.

The earl's commitments in the Midlands presumably meant that a holiday home in Worthing was surplus to requirements. It is possible too that, with a French invasion of England an ever-present threat, a house just a few hundred yards from the Sussex shoreline felt a vulnerable location for a member of the British nobility. Either way, the earl sold the estate on 21 August 1795 to Major John William Commerell for £2,920-10s.

Although the grounds of the house – which were the same in 1890 (see the plan on page 21) as they were in Jane Austen's time – were reasonably extensive, covering about six acres, much of the estate consisted of various parcels of land elsewhere in the central part of Worthing. These picturesquely named plots of land were listed in the 1795 conveyance and included Soapers Plot (sometimes Sopers Platt), the old field that was by then the garden of Warwick House; Maddocks Orchard, which became the paddock and shrubbery to the east of the house;

The Colonnade and Warwick House

The earlier version of this engraving of the Colonnade and Warwick House, above, which is dated 14 December 1804, shows no continuation of the terrace at the left of the picture, thus indicating that the houses on the north side of Warwick Street (see illustration on page 16) had not yet been built. The 1814 version, below, adds this continuation, and also shows that the building on the left of Warwick House, in which the kitchen was located, had now been joined to the house. The bell in the bell-tower was rung to summon the family to meals and – in an era when there was no public clock in Worthing, and few owned watches – its ringing at lunch-time told the townspeople that it was one o'clock.

Above: Warwick Street
Most of the houses on the north side of Warwick Street were built from about 1806 onwards, and, as this engraving shows, they originally had attractive and uniform bow fronts. Stanford's Cottage, where Jane Austen stayed in 1805, was (and is) set back from the left-hand side of the street, about a third of the way along.

Left: Warwick House in 1824
This engraving of Warwick House first appeared in 1824 in *A Topographical Description of Worthing* by John Shearsmith, who was a doctor in the town.

Long Croft; and Mole Soals. Also conveyed to Commerell was 'the pew late of John Luther in Broadwater Church'.[6]

Five years later – the conveyance is dated 25 March 1801 – Commerell sold the Warwick House estate to Edward Ogle for £5,000.[7] Ogle made further improvements, and 'at different times expended very considerable sums of money in enlarging and adorning [the house], and in the formation of pleasure grounds, walks, and shrubberies'.[8]

Worthing's architecture up to that point – and indeed subsequently – was mostly modest, particularly in comparison with the splendours of Brighton ten miles to the east. As a result, Warwick House seems to have been regarded with great pride in Worthing. John Evans, writing in *A Picture of Worthing* in 1805 – with the excessive use of commas often characteristic of the period – says:

> Warwick House, opposite the Colonnade Library, may, from its size, appearance, and situation, be ranked among the first habitations, in the kingdom, let as a marine residence: its present proprietor is Edward Ogle, Esq.; but during the season it is occupied by some family of distinction.

Evans's view may not be entirely objective, since it is likely that Ogle encouraged him to write *A Picture of Worthing* to serve as a semi-official guide-book to the town. In the 'Advertisement' at the start – although the book's publication date was 1805, the preface is dated 1 December 1804 – Evans tells us that he had spent the month of July in Worthing. He also writes that 'to one Gentleman in particular he begs leave thus publicly to return thanks for his obliging communications' while he was writing the book, and in all likelihood this gentleman was Ogle. Evans was the long-serving pastor of a congregation of Baptists in Worship Street in Hackney, only a mile north of Ralph's Quay, the wharf owned by the Ogle brothers, so he and Edward Ogle probably knew each other in London. If not, they would certainly have come across each other in Worthing that July.

John Evans (1767–1827) was a distinguished man. As well as being a Baptist minister, he was the 'master of a seminary for a limited number of pupils' in Pullin's Row, Islington and the author of about forty books. Some were modest volumes similar to his Worthing book, such as *An Excursion to Windsor* and *A Sail down the River Medway*. However he also wrote numerous more substantial works, most notably *A Sketch of the Denominations of the Christian World / Accompanied with a Persuasive to Religious Moderation / To Which is Prefixed an Account of Atheism, Deism, Theophilanthropism, Judaism, Mahometanism, and Christianity / Adapted to the Present Times*. This book of some three hundred pages, first published in 1797, went through at least eighteen editions in England and America, and was still being published in updated versions as late as 1841.

The pseudonymous poet Paul Potion,[9] who in 1814 published a 102-page poem in rhyming couplets entitled *A Poetical Picture of Worthing, and Its Vicinity / With an Introductory Description of the Route from the Metropolis* – this was, as Potion makes clear, in effect a verse version of Evans's book – also sang the praises of Warwick House:

> Just opposite the *Colonnade*
> Stands *Warwick House*, in gay parade;
> Which from its scale, may surely boast
> Itself the pride of England's coast!
> Nor must the reader here forget
> It is *occasionally* let;

To such as wear *the coronet*!
And may be justly ranked I ween,
A handsome *residence marine*.
Although the lower story be,
Encircled with a shrubbery,
From every room the eye will see,
Commanding prospects of the main,
And landscapes, truly *Claude Lorain*![10]

Ogle's adversary John Mackoull is less complimentary about the house, writing in the 1813 edition of his *A Sketch of Worthing*: 'From the outward appearance there is every thing to recommend it, but the internal accommodations fall very short of what might be expected.' He adds that the house is generally let to some 'noble personage' during the season, though rarely for long, owing either to the 'extravagant price' charged or to 'some other cause'.

Even if we attribute Mackoull's comments to prejudice, the suggestion made by Evans and Potion that the size and scale of Warwick House made it one of the finest marine residences 'in the kingdom' and 'the pride of England's coast' is not supported by the reality. The house, although pleasant and sunny – and in a prominent position, with a very attractive outlook – would not have seemed particularly grand except in early Worthing. On the ground floor the house had a fine dining room (thirty feet by twenty feet), together with a morning room, a smoking room, a large hall with a wide staircase, and the usual domestic offices – kitchen, housekeeper's room, butler's pantry and bedroom, and so on. On the first floor there were six principal bed and dressing rooms, three servants' bedrooms approached by a second staircase and – the house's chief glory – a drawing room of the same dimensions as the dining room below, with magnificent views south to the seafront across what is now Steyne Gardens, but at the start of the nineteenth century was simply a field. With no buildings to the east, there was also an uninterrupted view to Beachy Head. Above was an attic floor with a front-facing window and balcony.[11]

Nonetheless, although its size was relatively modest compared to the houses of the nearby Sussex estates such as Offington and Muntham, Warwick House was the most important house in the town, and its owner acquired much status from the fact of ownership.

In those days the owners of houses in sea-side towns often vacated them during the season for the profitable business of renting them to visiting nobility or gentlefolk, and during the period of Ogle's ownership many distinguished people stayed at Warwick House, a fact advertised by both Evans and Potion, as we have seen. During the summer months Ogle and his wife Ann relocated to a smaller house nearby. A scurrilous poem pinned up in Steyne Field in September 1812 (see page 29) indicates that their summer residence was in Bedford Row, a couple of minutes' walk away, although Ogle would also sometimes have been in London, attending to the businesses he ran with his brother.

The most notable summer occupant of Warwick House during Edward Ogle's time was Princess Charlotte, the eleven-year-old grand-daughter of George III and second in line to the throne, who spent a holiday there in July and August 1807. Princess Charlotte was much loved by the British people, during a period when the monarchy was otherwise far from popular. Had she not died in childbirth – on 6 November 1817, less than four months after Jane Austen – she would have succeeded her father George IV to the throne in 1830, and Britain would have had a Charlottean instead of a Victorian age.

Princess Charlotte arrived in Worthing with a large retinue on 21 July 1807. The streets of the town were festooned with flowers and lined by the part-time soldiers of the local volunteers, whose bands played. That evening the young princess, already schooled in the ways of royalty, appeared in the window of Warwick House to acknowledge the crowd, and the seafront was illuminated in her honour.

The honoured guest was celebrated everywhere in the town, and at one performance at the town's newly opened theatre an actor called William Oxberry recited a dreadful piece of doggerel entitled *Peeping Tom's Peep into Worthing*, which included lines in tribute to Princess Charlotte that were to prove sadly ironic:

> Warwick House is a place I much joy'd at beholding,
> Long life to the royal sweet blossom it's holding.[12]

On 10 August the princess's father, George, Prince of Wales – who from 1811 to 1820 was the Prince Regent – rode over from Brighton on horseback to see her. All this royal activity was a heady cocktail for the fledgling town, and the visit proved more beneficial to Worthing than a previous royal visit, by the Prince of Wales's sister Princess Amelia, who stayed for four months in 1798, although that too had been helpful in promoting the town.

The intention was that Princess Charlotte should stay at Warwick House again the following year, but 'for private reasons which it were here unnecessary to state' she went instead to Bognor.[13] The reason may have been that Edward Ogle had found a tenant who wanted the house for the entire summer rather than just a few weeks, since on 4 July 1808 the local newspaper reported: 'Worthing has become exceedingly gay. Warwick House has undergone repairs, been elegantly decorated, and has been engaged for three months by the Duke and Duchess of Montrose.'[14]

Another notable summer tenant of Warwick House during its – and Worthing's – glory years under Edward Ogle was Lord Mountjoy, later the Earl of Blessington, who had 'under his protection' Mrs Mary Brown, the lively and attractive young wife of an army officer who had been posted to the West Indies. General gossip left little doubt about the nature of the relationship and, after Captain Brown's death in 1812, Mountjoy married the widow, who herself died only two years later.

On Edward Ogle's death in 1819, the Warwick House estate passed to his brother James. Although James Ogle had some involvement in Edward's Worthing affairs, he always lived in London – in 1810 he was in Walthamstow[15] – and he never occupied the house he inherited from his brother. In a document of 1820 he is shown as a freeholder in Worthing, but his 'abode' is given as London.[16]

During the five years he owned Warwick House, James Ogle let it to a succession of rich and mostly titled visitors. The 6th Duke of Bedford was there in 1820. For six weeks in February and March 1822 the 3rd Earl of Warwick rented the house that his father had owned at the end of the previous century. The beautiful and famous actress Harriet Mellon – who at that time was the first wife of Thomas Coutts of the banking dynasty, and later married the Duke of St Albans – stayed at the house during April 1823, and returned for the months of July and August. The Hon. Henry Grey Bennet MP, a man described by his friend Thomas Creevey as 'most amiable, occasionally most boring', stayed for over six months, from the start of November 1823 to mid-May 1824. Other tenants of Warwick House during this period included the 4th Duke of Newcastle and the 5th Duke of Marlborough.

After James's death in 1824, Warwick House and its grounds were left to his eldest son James William,[17] and the copyhold lands belonging to the estate, including Steyne Gardens, to his widow Sarah, who thereafter lived in a house in the Colonnade. When Sarah Ogle died, the land she owned in Worthing went to her daughter Elizabeth, who sold Steyne Gardens in 1883 to George Whiffen, thus finally severing the Ogle family's eighty-year connection with the town.

James Ogle's son, James William, initially failed to find a buyer for Warwick House, and it was rented for six weeks in the summer of 1825 by the Bishop of Durham, the Rt Revd Shute Barrington (1734–1826), a man already in his nineties. The bishop liked the house so much that he then bought it with all its furniture for £12,000, with the intention of spending his retirement there. He ordered various alterations, and these took place during late 1825 and early 1826, but before he could take up permanent residence he died, in March 1826. Warwick House was bequeathed, together with an annuity of £1,000, to Anne Elizabeth Colberg (or Coburg), who had been a companion to him and his wife for twenty-five years; but she never lived there, and in due course sold the house to General Sir Richard Jones, who, like Ogle, seems to have continued Ogle's practice of renting out the house in the summer.

General Jones had retired to Worthing in 1810 after a long military career in India, so his association with the town went back to the Edward Ogle era. Indeed in 1813 he had served with Ogle on a small committee looking into problems with Worthing's finances. It is not clear when he acquired Warwick House, but his ownership ended in February 1835 after his post-boy drove his post-chaise – these were small, light, fast-moving carriages – into a pond near Angmering Station. The 83-year-old general did not recover from the shock of being immersed in ice-cold water, and died soon afterwards. His widow continued to occupy the house for a while, and it seems then to have remained in the Jones family for the rest of its existence, although none of its members lived there again.

With the Napoleonic Wars over, the wealthy and fashionable were again spending their holidays on the continent of Europe. In addition there was much competition from other English seaside resorts for diminishing trade. As a result, by 1829 Worthing found itself virtually bankrupt, and this dismal situation continued through most of the 1830s. Warwick House was not immune from the effects of this decline in the town's economy. At a parish meeting on 16 May 1836 it was stated that, while in the 1820s the house was being let for £25 a week, now no tenant could be found who was willing to pay even £8 – and that for fifteen months it had not been let at all.

Worthing never recovered the status it had had at the start of the century. Fashionable visitors were going elsewhere, and as the years passed Warwick House stood empty for long periods. Tenants were intermittently found, but the names are more modest than in the house's heyday: Captain and Mrs Tinling (1849–50), J.B. Fletcher (1857), William Tollemarche (1859). Later there were longer lets: the Misses Byrom were at Warwick House from 1870 to 1873, and Mrs Nicholls from 1874 to 1883.

From 1884 on Warwick House was unoccupied. In 1887 it was suggested that the town should buy it to create a public library, museum and art school, and that its attractive grounds should be preserved as a public amenity in the heart of Worthing. But nothing came of this idea and the house lay in limbo for a further decade.

During this final period of near-dereliction illuminated promenade concerts were regularly held in the grounds in the summer – as, for example, on 1 August 1894, when the Band of the Royal Marine Artillery played. The band was described as 'a skilled body of musicians, whose efforts were regarded as generally acceptable', but 'exception was taken in some quarters to the composition of the programme, which, it was declared, was not altogether suited to the occasion'. The unsuitable programme included Haydn's *Austrian Hymn* and selections from *The Gondoliers* and *The Mikado*, as well as now-forgotten pieces such as Godfrey's *Reminiscences of England*, Lindpaintner's overture *The Foster Children*, and Pougher's *Reminiscences of Tosti*. Refreshments were provided by the Aerated Bread Company.[18]

These melancholy musical events were Warwick House's swansong. It is not altogether surprising that the house, however attractive its setting, could not find a buyer. It had an awkward status, having something of the character of a small country house while being

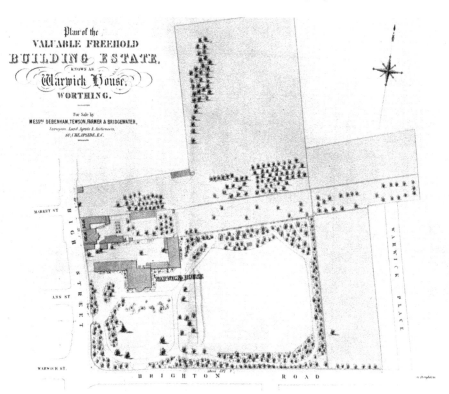

The Grounds of Warwick House
This plan of Warwick House and its grounds dates from 1890. The extent of the grounds was much the same at the start of the nineteenth century as here, although there would have been fewer mature trees.

Warwick House in 1790
This view of Warwick House was painted by S. H. Grimm (1733–1794) about five years after the house was built.

situated immediately adjacent to the heart of a busy town that was rapidly increasing in size (in 1801 the population of Worthing and Broadwater had been 2,151; by 1901 it was 24,479). By the standards of a house with pretensions to grandeur, the grounds of Warwick House were relatively small, and the house itself was by now old-fashioned and outdated. It needed considerable modernisation, and there was still no bathroom. In addition Worthing, which had during the first two decades of the nineteenth century been a quieter alternative to Brighton for the rich and fashionable, had long been a more humdrum location, and 'Warwick House, Worthing' would no longer have been a particularly impressive address.

Moreover, rich Victorian industrialists and entrepreneurs had little interest in taking on old-fashioned houses such as Warwick House, preferring to build vast, confident modern mansions to their own specifications. Indeed, had its grounds been bigger, the fate of Warwick House might have been to be demolished to make way for a late-Victorian pile. However no private purchaser came forward to restore or replace it, and in the end it was a builder called Ephraim Kellett who bought the house and the grounds in 1896.

The house was demolished, and most of the grounds were used for conventional housing, on roads that Kellett laid out – Elm Road, Warwick Gardens, Ash Grove and Wyke Avenue. Kellett also built himself a new, more modest Warwick House, which still stands in Warwick Gardens.

On the front garden of the old house was erected – in 1901 – an unusual and striking building, which has already dominated the northern end of Steyne Gardens for longer than Warwick House did. At street level there are shops, and above are flats, many of whose windows have the same magnificent view across Steyne Gardens to the sea that was enjoyed from the first-floor drawing room of Warwick House by Edward and Ann Ogle – and, almost certainly, by Jane Austen too.

Chapter 2
Edward Ogle – The Inspiration for 'Mr Parker'

Edward Ogle – on whom the character of Tom Parker in *Sanditon* is based – and his brother James were the two sons of James and Mary Ogle, *née* Park, who also had four daughters: Judith (later Drabble), who seems to have died before Edward wrote his will in 1809, since she is not mentioned in it; Sarah (later Hall); Elizabeth (later Collin); and Mary, who was still a spinster at the time of Edward's will.[1]

The Ogles came from the north of England. Members of the Ogle family had been prominent landed gentry in Northumberland from before the time of the Norman Conquest, and Edward Ogle's parents were married in the small market town of Rothbury, twenty-six miles north of Newcastle, on 13 October 1748. It was also in Rothbury that their sons were baptised.

Two surviving documents that provide evidence as to which of Edward and James was the elder are at variance, but the more persuasive indicates that it was James. This is the 1835 affidavit of George Ogle, James's youngest son, in which he refers to Edward as the second son of his grandparents. Attached to this affidavit is an abstract from the Rothbury parish register stating that James's baptism took place on 16 May 1757 and Edward's on 15 May 1759. This abstract – which includes the formula 'The above are true copies of the Register Books of Marriages and Baptisms of the Parish of Rothbury' – was signed on 30 January 1835 by both the curate and the vestry clerk, so it is unlikely that the brothers' baptism dates were transposed.[2]

Puzzlingly, however, a Deed Poll of Declaration by James's 'widow and relict' Sarah on 1 October 1825 refers to 'Edward Ogle formerly of Warwick House deceased' as 'the elder brother of the said James Ogle'.[3] It cannot be that Sarah did not know whether or not her husband was older than his only brother. It seems therefore that in 1825 Sarah untruthfully asserted Edward's seniority in order to facilitate some provision in James's will that could not be put into effect on account of poorly drafted earlier documentation, since the Deed Poll concerns the renunciation by Sarah Ogle of trusts specified in Edward's will. Indeed it was probably as the consequence of Sarah's false statement that – in order to resolve some subsequent testamentary problem – George Ogle found it necessary ten years later to ask Rothbury parish to provide the cast-iron proof that his father James had indeed been the elder.

A final pointer to James's having been the elder brother comes from an entry in the *London Gazette* in June 1793 concerning 'the partnership lately subsisting between James Ogle, Edward Ogle and Edward Joseph Mallough, of Ralph's Quay', which had been dissolved on 25 March that year. James's name comes first, out of alphabetical order, not only in the text but also in the sequence of the three signatories' names at the bottom.

Edward Ogle's wife, Ann, born in 1758, was the fourth daughter of Edmund Elsden, a merchant of Lynn (now King's Lynn) in Norfolk and his wife Elizabeth.[4] Elsden dealt in sand and Baltic timber, some of the sand being shipped to London for his customers, including the Staffordshire potter John Baddeley, who sourced his supplies through London dealers. Lynn sand was also, as Josiah Wedgwood notes, used at the famous Bow porcelain factory.[5] In view of the fact that the Ogle brothers kept a wharf on the Thames, it is probable that it was through the two families' connections with maritime trade that Ann Elsden met Edward Ogle. Edward and Ann, the date of whose marriage cannot be traced, had no children.[6] James and his wife Sarah, whom he married 'on or about 6 December 1788' at St John's church, Hackney,[7] had nine.

James and Edward Ogle were the partners in the firm of Messrs Ogle and Company, which had a warehouse and a wharf at Ralph's Quay. This was in a prime position on Lower Thames Street, on the north bank of the Thames four hundred yards east of London Bridge, a site now occupied by the Custom House. Two hundred years before, in 1603, Ralph's Quay had been described as 'one of the fairest by the Thames side'.[8] On 24 July 1795 James, then of Stoke Newington, and Edward, then of Upper Clapton, made a routine application to license no fewer than nine Thames barges – one of which was called *Brothers* – so Messrs Ogle and Company was clearly a substantial business. The 'area of navigation' of the Ogle barges is given as between Ralph's Quay and Deptford.[9]

To judge from the transcript of a trial held at the Old Bailey on 15 April 1801 – just three weeks after Edward Ogle bought Warwick House – one of the firm's main businesses was the import of sugar from the West Indies. A man called John-Henry Wackerbarth was tried 'for feloniously receiving, on the 16th of July, two thousand five hundred pounds weight of sugar', worth £100, from one 'Peter Perry, alias Parry', who had been found guilty of the theft itself at an earlier trial. The sugar in question was the 'sweepings and drainings' left after the shipment had left the warehouse. Edward Ogle gave detailed evidence. After stating that he had been a 'wharfinger' – that is, the keeper or owner of a wharf – for fourteen or fifteen years, he explained

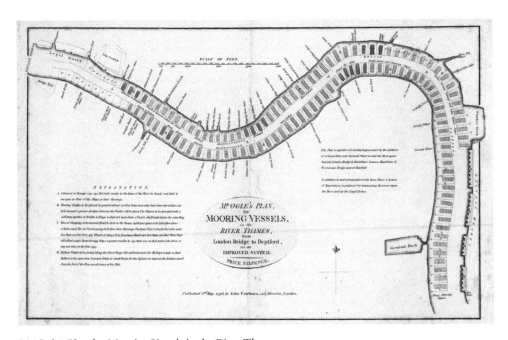

Mr Ogle's Plan for Mooring Vessels in the River Thames
Edward Ogle's 1796 proposal for a new system for organising river traffic on the Thames was an attempt to solve the problem of overcrowding caused by the doubling of London's seaborne trade since 1760. In the event his suggestion was passed over in favour of the more ambitious West India Docks and Wapping Docks schemes. (© National Maritime Museum, London)

West India Docks
This is a view of the five-storey warehouses at the Import Dock, which opened in 1802. The Import Dock was the first of three docks built on the Isle of Dogs after Edward Ogle's scheme for reorganising the mooring arrangements on the Thames was rejected. The picture, a collaboration between Augustus Charles Pugin (born 1762, 1768 or 1769, died 1832) and Thomas Rowlandson (1757–1827), was first published in 1810. (Yale Center for British Art)

what usually happened to the sugar left behind on the warehouse floor: 'The wharfinger is to dispose of the sweepings and drainings if he pleases, or he may give them to his clerk in order to keep the warehouses clean; if that was not to be done the warehouses would be knee deep.' Asked, 'Are these warehouses, which you say but for this would be knee deep, yours?', Ogle replied that they were. In the event Wackerbarth was found not guilty.[10]

Edward Ogle had also been at the Old Bailey two months earlier, on 18 February 1801, for the trial of two men, Abraham Davidson and Thomas Ferguson, on the charge of 'feloniously stealing, on the 19th of January, a coil of rope, value 39s. the property of James and Edward Ogle'. Again, the men were acquitted.[11] It is telling that, although James was the elder brother, it was Edward who spoke at both these hearings.

The Ogles' warehouse must have been one of those that burnt down in the major fire at Ralph's Quay on 14 May 1809, which destroyed 'the entire stack' of warehouses between the quay and the street, as well as some ships. The magnitude of the event can be gauged from the fact that the cost of the damage was £75,000 – a huge sum (the insurance cover ran to only £25,000). To judge from the goods destroyed in the fire, the Ogles' business may have involved – in addition to the import of sugar – the export or import of bacon, butter, tallow, hides and salt-petre, a substance used for curing meat.[12]

Messrs Ogle and Company was not the Ogle brothers' only business. They were also the partners in the firm of James & Edward Ogle & Co, Ship & Insurance Brokers, of New City Chambers, Bishopsgate Street. (The sequencing of the brothers' names in this firm's title provides yet further evidence that James was the elder.) In his capacity as a partner in this firm Edward was in correspondence in 1806–7 with James Monroe – at that time the American Minister to the Court of St James, but later to be the fifth president of the United States – in connection with the illegal Spanish seizure of some American ships. On 27 March 1806 Edward Ogle wrote to say that various London underwriters were 'distressed' (in other words, had suffered serious losses) as a result of the illegal seizures and were looking for compensation for the stolen ships and their cargoes. On 16 December 1806, Ogle requested a meeting with Monroe to discuss the underwriters' concerns. There is no record of whether or not the meeting took place, but it is reasonable to assume that it did, since a third letter, of 10 February 1807, set out the claims in detail.[13]

Edward Ogle was also the Chairman of the Committee of Proprietors of the Legal Quays, in which capacity he was one of the most important figures in London's docklands. In London, as later in Worthing, he was a man of initiative and ideas. In 1796 he submitted a detailed proposal for re-organising the shipping entering the Thames, *Mr Ogle's Plan for Mooring Vessels in the River Thames*. The Pool of London at that time was cluttered and disorganised, and Ogle suggested that vessels should be moored according to their country of departure and the type of cargo they carried. He believed that his plan would help the port cope with the growing amount of river traffic, but it was not in the end used, the enclosed docks being built instead. Ogle was, however, reimbursed the sum of £253-12-7 for his expenses.[14]

A final piece of evidence that gives an indication of the Ogle brothers' wealth and importance in London's docklands was the size of their investment in the City Canal project. This ambitious scheme, authorised by the West India Docks Act of 1799, connected the two stretches of the Thames either side of the Isle of Dogs, providing sailing ships with a short cut to the wharves in the upper reaches of the river, including the Ogle wharf near London Bridge. The Ogle brothers' 6,000 shares made them the largest shareholders in the project apart from the Mayor of London, the Commonality and the Citizens of the City, which jointly held 29,000. The canal, which was about two-thirds of a mile in length, sixty yards wide and forty-five feet deep, was completed in 1805, but it was not a financial success, since its owners did not charge tolls; and it was sold in 1829 to the West India Dock Company, owner of the adjacent West India Docks.

By the start of the nineteenth century Edward Ogle was seeking a new challenge, and the fact that Warwick House was on the market presented that opportunity. A visit to Worthing would have indicated that the village was stirring into life, and it is safe to assume that Ogle bought the Warwick House estate as much for the development potential afforded by the lands that went with it as for the pleasure of living in an attractive and elegant house three hundred yards from the sea-shore. He was almost forty-two when he came to Worthing, which thereafter occupied much of his energy, so it is probable that James then shouldered more of the burden of the family businesses in London than before. Edward Ogle's contribution to the development of Worthing will be explored in Chapter 6.

Edward Ogle was not only a highly successful businessman, but also – and the two do not always go together – an upright man with strong moral principles. The brothers' involvement in the sugar trade with the West Indies would have made them well-informed on the subject of slavery, to which they were strongly opposed. They were among the subscribers to an important book called *The Interesting Narrative of the Life of Olaudah Equiano, or Gustavus Vassa, the African*. This vivid account of the suffering involved in slavery, first published in 1789, was highly influential in fuelling the growing anti-slavery movement in Britain. Among the other subscribers were the Prince of Wales – whose daughter Princess Charlotte was, as we saw in Chapter 1, later to be a summer tenant of Edward Ogle's at Warwick House – John Wesley and Josiah Wedgwood.

In more parochial matters Edward Ogle also was on the side of propriety and decent behaviour, as is testified by this brief report in the *The Sussex Weekly Advertiser, or Lewes and Brighthelmston Journal* on 29 August 1808:

> At a sitting of Magistrates at Steyning, a few days since, George Chipper, of West Tarring, was convicted on the complaint of Edward Ogle, esq. of driving his cart very furiously on the public road, to the great danger and annoyance of several ladies of Worthing. It is hoped this will deter others from the dangerous practice of driving carts violently on the road, to the great danger and terror of persons travelling thereon.

However Ogle's desire for order and control seems sometimes to have made him high-handed, and in the summer of 1812 the peace of Worthing was shattered by an acrimonious dispute that ended in an unseemly brawl. We know of these events from the 1813 edition of *A Sketch of Worthing* by Ogle's adversary John Mackoull, and we do not have Ogle's side of the story. However it is unlikely that Mackoull would have published complete untruths and, although his commentary on the events is filtered through personal prejudice, it is clear that Ogle was not universally popular in Worthing.

In his account of the matter Mackoull quotes from a daily newspaper's coverage of the story, although from its style and tone it is difficult to avoid the conclusion that Mackoull himself was the author of the newspaper report.

In the summer of 1812, a local band started performing in Steyne Field in the evenings, but, according to the report, their musicianship was poor:

> A puerile endeavour has been made to raise what was termed a band, but a more disgusting set of inharmonious dull bards we never witnessed; after annoying the company for several evenings with their discordant powers, they were very properly ordered to sound a retreat.

However the band of the South Bramber Volunteers then filled the breach. Their musicianship was of a higher standard, and every evening they played 'some excellent pieces of music' on Steyne Field. This 'gave offence to a very *great* man ycleped [called] *King Ogle*, who opposed the minstrels *tooth* and *nail*'. The reason that Ogle objected was probably that in his view loud music spoiled the quiet enjoyment of Worthing by its distinguished summer visitors, not least whoever was occupying Warwick House that season. So Ogle put up the following notice:

> MR JOHN DAVISON,
>
> I do hereby give you notice, that if at any time *hereafter*, you come upon the land called the *Steyne*, lying in Worthing, in the parish of Broadwater, in the county of Sussex, for any *purpose whatever*, I shall consider you a *wilful trespasser*, and an action will be brought against you accordingly. Witness my hand, the twelfth day of September, 1812.
>
>   EDWARD OGLE

Mackoull – he is now speaking for himself, rather than quoting from the newspaper report – says that 'the ridiculous absurdity of such a notice, indicating an irascible temper, excited a degree of warmth on the part of the mal-contents'. Someone – again one assumes Mackoull's authorship – then composed a satirical poem entitled 'Music Mania, or, A St Cecilian Ode', and

Worthing Seafront in August 1818 (West)
In the centre of this pencil-sketch are Montpelier Terrace and Montague Terrace. The low building that follows is Wicks's Baths, to the right of which are Bath Buildings, the Sea House Inn and the New Inn. At the far right is Stafford's Marine Library.

Worthing Seafront in August 1818 (East)
The buildings are, from left to right: Little Terrace; Bedford Row; Stafford's Library and Rebecca House; the Steyne Hotel and Steyne Row; and, behind the final boat, the Colonnade.

pinned it up opposite Ogle's notice. The author is given as Benjamin Bagpipe, his location as Mount Etna, and the date as 16 September 1812.

Bagpipe's poem is not always easy to follow, but its gist is that the poet is encouraging the 'South Bramber Music Madders', as he terms them, to continue playing in spite of the objections of 'the mighty monarch *of the land*' – who apparently goes about the town with a large Newfoundland mastiff. Although the dog '*looks* a little bold', it is in fact 'getting rather old' and loud music makes it urinate.[15] Bagpipe says that Ogle sends John Skewen – this was John Snewin, manager of the Warwick House estate[16] – to spy on the band, while he himself remains in Bedford Row, which is where he seems to have occupied a house while Warwick House was let out in the summer months. There, according to Bagpipe, Ogle sits 'stewing highly' (anxiously fretting) and 'drinking swipes' (weak inferior beer). Bagpipe says that this beer-drinking gives Ogle stomach pains, which he tries to alleviate by drinking large quantities of 'rue tea' and 'surfeit-water' (liquids prescribed after over-indulgence). As a result of drinking these cordials, 'wind escapes, and such like matter – loosely'. (This of course was the Regency age, when scatological satire was much in vogue.) Bagpipe ends his poem by saying that Mr Abbot, a haberdasher from Berners Street in London who is holidaying in Worthing, is so incensed by Ogle's attempt to stop the band playing that he has sworn that if 'the King' and his dog pass his lodgings in Warwick Street he will horsewhip them both.

For the climax of the story we return to the newspaper report from which Mackoull quotes:

> The *sabbath-day* was considered by him [Ogle] as the most appropriate for hostilities. Peace on earth, and good-will towards men, was obliterated from the mind, while the unhallowed principles of ill-nature and revenge reigned predominant. To hard words succeeded blows, and the Steyne became a scene of uproar and confusion that beggars all description, until the giant [Ogle] made a retrograde movement [retreated], the band playing 'Get out of my sight or I'll box your ears'. It is said that this row will occasion a reference to the Court of King's Bench.

Presumably the matter did not actually reach the courts, but it must have afforded much amusement to those citizens of Worthing that were not directly involved.

Edward Ogle died at some point in March 1819,[17] and his will – which had been drawn up on 18 March 1809 – was proved on 26 May of that year. It is a long and complicated document, the probate copy running to ten closely written pages. Ogle left to his 'beloved and affectionate wife Ann' the couple's china and glass, together with her own 'paraphernalia, wearing apparel and linen and all her watches, rings, trinkets and jewels'. (To the modern eye it seems curious that Ann had to have her own clothes and valuables left to her in her husband's will.) The 'wines and liquors' at Warwick House were left jointly to Ann and to his brother James. Ann was to be responsible for dividing these up into equal shares by value, and the ever-punctilious Ogle asked her to take account of the quality of the various wines to ensure that the division by value was done fairly. Ann was also to receive £500 immediately on her husband's death, and a substantial annuity of £1,050. Warwick House, its grounds and most of what was left of the rest of the estate – much had already been sold and built upon – were, as we saw in Chapter 1, bequeathed to James.[18]

Ann Ogle died less than five years after her husband, on 8 January 1824,[19] and James Ogle died the same year. John Shearsmith, writing soon after James Ogle's death, is complimentary about his character:

Upon the death of Mr. Ogle, [Warwick House] became the property of his brother James Ogle, Esq. a gentleman held in much estimation for his politeness and urbanity, but who did not long enjoy it, having recently been destined to share the lot incidental to our mortal nature.[20]

Perhaps the reference to James's politeness and urbanity and the lack of any comment about Edward hold the implication that the latter was not held in quite so much 'estimation' by the people of Worthing as his brother. Or perhaps it is simply that Shearsmith was concentrating his attention on speaking well of a man who had just died. Either way, as in the case of most driven and ambitious men, Edward Ogle was clearly someone who divided opinion.

Worthing Point, from Shoreham
Just visible in the background of this print of 1818 is the promontory that existed at Worthing in the early nineteenth century.

Chapter 3

Jane Austen's Visit to Worthing

Before we embark on our account of Jane Austen's stay in Worthing in 1805, we need briefly to set the visit in the context of her life.[1]

Jane Austen's father, George Austen, was the rector of Steventon in Hampshire. He and his wife, Cassandra Leigh Austen, had eight children – six sons and two daughters, the daughters being Cassandra, the fifth child, and Jane, the seventh. Cassandra remained Jane's closest friend and confidante throughout her life, and, like Jane, she never married. She died in 1845 at the age of seventy-two, outliving her famous sister by nearly twenty-eight years.

Jane was always at her happiest when her routine was orderly. During the second half of the 1790s she was living at Steventon in Hampshire with her parents and sister, and her writing had flowed, including early versions of the novels that were later published as *Sense and Sensibility*, *Northanger Abbey* and *Pride and Prejudice*. By comparison, most of the first decade of the nineteenth century was less productive.

In December 1800 George Austen, by then in his late sixties, decided to hand over the parish to his eldest son James and move to Bath with his wife and daughters. Cassandra was almost twenty-eight, and Jane had just turned twenty-five. The decision to leave Steventon was sudden, and came as a shock to Jane, who returned from a visit to her friend Martha Lloyd – who was to be a member of the party in Worthing five years later – to be told that the family was to leave their house a week later.

Thus began a period of eight and a half years that were often semi-nomadic in character. Although the family was nominally resident in Bath between 1800 and George Austen's death in January 1805, much of its time was spent elsewhere. In particular their father loved visiting the seaside resorts of Dorset and Devon, and Cassandra and Jane accompanied their parents. Jane had therefore had no alternative but to accustom herself to an irregular existence.

This was just as well, because after her father died, it was no longer a matter of choice but of necessity that she, her sister and their mother were often of no fixed abode. They were adequately well off – Mrs Austen and Cassandra had a little money of their own, and most of Mrs Austen's sons provided some financial assistance – but they lacked the security provided by a settled home.

For the first part of the summer of 1805, from mid-June onwards, Mrs Austen and her two daughters were at Godmersham Park in Kent, the home of her third son, Edward – and the stay in Worthing came after this.

Then from October 1806 to April 1809 the Austen ladies lived in Southampton, where they shared two successive rented houses with Mrs Austen's fifth son, Frank, a naval officer, and his first wife. Martha Lloyd had by then become a permanent part of Mrs Austen's household. The Austen and Lloyd families had known each other for many years, and Jane had become particularly close to Martha, whose mother died on 16 April 1805. Martha's joining the Austen household was partly from reasons of friendship and partly because it made sense to all of them to combine expenses. She remained unmarried until in 1828, aged sixty-two, she became she second wife of Jane's brother Frank.

Mrs Austen's household finally acquired a permanent home in the summer of 1809. This was provided for them by her son Edward.

At the age of 12, Edward had had the good fortune to catch the eye of Thomas and Catherine Knight, who were rich, childless relations of his father's. The Knights took a close interest in Edward and eventually adopted him. After Thomas Knight's death in 1794, Edward became the owner not only of Godmersham Park (in which Catherine Knight retained a life interest) but also of estates at Steventon and Chawton.

In 1809 Edward offered his mother and sisters a choice of two houses – one at Godmersham, the other at Chawton. They opted for the latter, and moved into Chawton Cottage in July 1809. Jane Austen remained there for the rest of her life, with the exception of the final two months, when Cassandra and their brother Henry took their dying sister to Winchester for better medical treatment; and it was there that she died in July 1817. The four of Jane Austen's novels that appeared in her lifetime were all published during the eight years she lived at Chawton.

...

The visit to Worthing came in the middle of the particularly unsettled period of almost two years immediately after George Austen's death. The town was a new destination for the Austen ladies, and we do not know why they decided to go there. However, as we shall see, Mrs Austen and Martha Lloyd preceded Jane and Cassandra to Worthing – possibly by as much as seven weeks – so it is likely that it was Mrs Austen that was the driving force behind the arrangement. Although she was to outlive her younger daughter by ten years, Mrs Austen worried incessantly about her health, so she probably decided that she would benefit from the restorative properties of a spell at the seaside.

The first reference to the proposal that Cassandra and Jane should stay in Worthing comes in a letter from Jane to her sister on Saturday 24 August 1805. Jane is staying with Edward and his wife Elizabeth at Godmersham Park, while Cassandra is sixteen miles away at Goodnestone Farm, where the Austen sisters' recently orphaned cousins, Fanny and Sophia Cage, were living with Lady Bridges. (Lady Bridges was the Cage sisters' grandmother and Elizabeth Austen's mother.) Jane mentions the trip to Worthing in relation to the fact that the eldest of Edward and Elizabeth's sons – also Edward, and then aged ten or eleven – is unwell:

> Little Edw[ard] is by no means better … Unless he recovers his strength beyond what is now probable, his brothers will return to School without him, & he will be of the party to Worthing. – If Sea-Bathing should be recommended he will be left there with us.[2]

On Monday 26 August Jane was taken to Canterbury in the Godmersham carriage, where she met up with Cassandra, who had driven there in the Goodnestone carriage. The sisters then swapped places, Cassandra proceeding to Godmersham and Jane to Goodnestone Farm, where she stayed until Monday 2 September.[3]

There is a second mention of the proposed trip to Worthing in a letter from Jane to Cassandra from Goodnestone on Friday 30 August. The arrangements for Worthing have been complicated by a visit that has now been planned by the two sisters to their brother Henry in London:

> The journey to London is a point of the first expediency, and I am glad it is resolved on. Though it seems likely to injure our Worthing scheme … We shall not be at Worthing so soon as we

View of Lancing on the Worthing Road to Brighton
Although this scene is a few miles to the east of Worthing, it gives a good impression of the quiet roads and scattered homesteads that were characteristic of the area in the early nineteenth century. This undated and unsigned hand-coloured etching probably dates from about 1820.

The Tollhouse at Teville Gate
The turnpike road to Worthing had been open only for a year or so at the time of Jane Austen's visit in 1805. The turnpike gate at Worthing, which was the third on the new road (the others were at Dial Post and Ashington), stood at the junction of Broadwater Road and Teville Road. Although only part of the notice on the side of the tollhouse is legible, it appears to be a warning to vagrants and thieves that they were not welcome in Worthing. The watercolour of *c*. 1805–10 is by John Nixon (*c*. 1750–1818).

Fanny Austen (1793–1882)
The letters and diaries of her niece Fanny give us the only direct information that we have about Jane Austen's 1805 stay in Worthing. This watercolour of Fanny was done by Jane's sister Cassandra on 3 September 1805, a fortnight before the three of them travelled to Worthing with Fanny's parents and her governess, Miss Sharpe. Mrs Austen and Martha Lloyd were already in the town. (© Jane Austen Memorial Trust)

have been used to talk of, shall we? This will be no evil to us, and we are sure of my mother and Martha being happy together.[4]

Although the final sentence makes clear that Mrs Austen and Martha Lloyd were already in Worthing, the date of their arrival there is not known. A letter written a month earlier – on Sunday 28 July – by Edward Austen's eldest child, Fanny, to her former governess, Miss Chapman, included the information that Mrs Austen was due to leave Godmersham 'on Wednesday' (that is, 31 July).[5] We do not know whether Mrs Austen then stayed somewhere else first, or went immediately to Worthing. Perhaps she met up somewhere with Martha Lloyd and travelled to Worthing with her; if not, Martha must have joined her there soon afterwards. Either way, Mrs Austen and Martha were in Worthing well before the others.

Jane's letter of 30 August also refers to news she has received from Godmersham, seemingly in a letter from her sister-in-law Elizabeth. 'Little Edward' is now better and will therefore probably be able to return to school with his younger brothers – as evidently proved to be the case, since he was not in the event a member of the party to Worthing.

This is the last letter that Jane Austen wrote that included any reference to the Worthing visit – and indeed it is the last surviving letter of hers until January 1807, if we exclude a poem she sent Fanny in July 1806.[6] Long intervals such as this in the letter record are one reason why there are many gaps in the chronology of Jane Austen's life; and when Cassandra was with her she was of course not writing to the person who was her most regular correspondent. We therefore have no direct information from Jane Austen about what she did in Worthing, and are almost entirely dependent on the diaries of Fanny Austen. Invaluable though these are, they tell us only about the initial six days during which Fanny and her parents stayed in the town.

(A note on nomenclature. Jane Austen's biographers usually refer to Fanny as Fanny Knight, which she became when her father changed the family surname in 1812. In 1805, however, she was Fanny Austen, and this was her name until she was nineteen. She was Fanny Knight for only eight years – she married in 1820, and for the remaining sixty-two years of her life she was Lady Knatchbull.)

Fanny's first mention of Worthing is in a letter of Sunday 15 September 1805 to her former governess, Miss Chapman:

Papa, Mama, Aunts C— and Jane, Miss Sharpe [Fanny's new governess] & myself set out on Tuesday for Worthing in Sussex, where Miss S will stay some time, for her eyes, but Papa, Mama, & I return in about a week, so that we shall be very happy to see you, on Friday or Saturday the 27th or 28th if it is convenient to you. If you do not write, we shall expect you on one of those days, if you do direct to [address your letter to] 'Mr Stanfords, Worthing, Shoreham,' & your letter will arrive safe. I enjoy the thoughts of sea-bathing very much.[7]

On Tuesday 17 September the party duly set off for Worthing. Fanny briefly describes the journey in her diary:[8]

Papa, Mama, Aunts Cass & Jane & I set off for Battel [Battle], where we arrived about 4, & finding no accommodations we proceeded to Horsebridge where we slept. (We saw the Abbey at Battel.)

The next day, Wednesday 18 September, the party – which also included Miss Sharpe – arrived in Worthing, where Mrs Austen and Martha Lloyd were already entrenched:

We proceeded for Worthing at 9, spent 2 or 3 hours at Brighton & arrived there at 5. We walked on the Sands in the evening.

On Thursday 19 September there was seaside and social activity:

I went with G-mama [Mrs Austen] in the morning to buy fish on the Beach, & afterwards with Mama & Miss Sharpe to Bathe where I had a most delicious dip. Mama & I called on Miss Fielding twice & she was not at home & afterwards she called on us. We dined at 4 & went to a Raffle in the evening, where Aunt Jane won & it amounted to 17– [seventeen shillings].

Friday 20 September was again active and sociable:

Mama & I [word illegible] some time with M— Fielding & I afterwards waited on the Sands for Aunt Cassandra coming out of the warm bath [this would have been Wicks's Warm Baths on the sea-front, at that time the only public baths in Worthing] & then walked with Mama, Jane & the Johnsons in the morning, when I was walking with G-mama & again in the evening. We went to the Raffle in the evening.

Saturday 21 September seems to have been a rather dull day:

Miss Fielding dined with us, & we did not walk in the evening. I called on the Johnsons.

And Sunday 22 September was duller still:

Morning Church. Miss Lloyd, G-mama, & Aunt Jane, went to Church, & I wrote Henry [one of Fanny's younger brothers].

The following day, Monday 23 September, Fanny and her parents left Worthing (Miss Sharpe remained):

Papa, Mama, & I set off from Worthing, to Hastings, where we arrived about 8 after many difficulties. We could get no horses for a long time at Seaford, & Southbourne.

It is intriguing to note from Fanny's diary that social interaction began the day after their arrival in Worthing. This does not seem to have been owing to Mrs Austen's having made friends in the town, since it is clearly Fanny and her mother that were already acquainted with Miss Fielding and the Johnsons – indeed, since they twice sought out Miss Fielding on their first full day in Worthing, she seems to have been a particular friend. Fanny's father, however, is notable by his absence from any of the social events to which Fanny refers. He is mentioned only on the day of their arrival and the day of their departure. The sole male in a party of seven, he presumably found something else to do.

An interesting element of Fanny's diary is the careful record that she keeps of her income and expenditure on the pages set aside for the purpose on the right-hand side. Tuesday was evidently her pocket money day, and beside every Tuesday in September is the entry '[received] of Mama' with the digit '6' in the column designated for pence. During the first week in September Fanny 'gave Boy' sixpence, but since she had sixpence 'in hand' at the start of the week, she was also able to spend fourpence on 'Seed' and still have twopence left at the end of the week. The following week she 'gave Boy' twopence, and that week's sixpence pocket money was also all spent, though Fanny does not specify on what. She therefore set off for Sussex on 17 September with no 'money in hand'. During the Worthing week her outgoings exactly matched her income: fivepence of her pocket money went to 'Pastry Cook' – Fanny must generously have bought

Wicks's Original Royal Baths
The building that appears to be just to the left of Wicks's Baths is Montpelier Terrace, built *c.* 1810 at the southern end of Montague Place, and therefore about eighty-five yards to the west of Wicks's Baths. This print probably dates from the early 1820s, since it shows the new seafront promenade, which was completed in 1821. Jane Austen's sister Cassandra patronised Wicks's Baths on 20 September 1805.

Fishermen Going on Board at Worthing
This dramatic painting of 1797 is the work of Philippe Jacques de Loutherbourg (1740–1812), who was born in Strasbourg, but moved to London in 1771.

Above: St Mary's, Broadwater
This engraving depicts the church that Jane Austen attended during her stay in 1805. It was situated a mile and a quarter north of the heart of Worthing. The short spire was taken down when the church was restored in 1826, but the old cottages in front survive, albeit much altered. This view is, like several other engravings in this book, the work of the prolific James Rouse of Fulham, who specialised in scenes of Sussex, many of which were collected in his books *Scraps of Sussex* (1817) and *The Beauties and Antiquities of the County of Sussex* (1825).

Left: Revd Peter Wood
Wood, who was Rector of Broadwater from 1797 to 1853, was known as 'the hunting parson' because he was apparently more at home on horseback than in the pulpit. It is certain that he met Jane Austen, since hers was one of the witness signatures on an affidavit that Martha Lloyd swore in front of him on 4 November 1805.

cakes and pastries for the whole party – and she 'gave Boy' a penny. So Fanny left Sussex as poor as she had arrived. Once she was back at Godmersham, she gave the mysterious 'Boy' nothing more. (Could Boy have been a pet bird, and 'gave' be Fanny's shorthand for expenses involved in his upkeep? This would explain her purchase of seed.)

After Fanny and her parents left on 23 September, Mrs Austen, Cassandra, Jane and Martha stayed at least a further six weeks, since they were certainly still in Worthing on Monday 4 November, on which date Martha swore an affidavit before the Rector of Broadwater in relation to her late mother's will, with Jane as one of the witnesses.[9]

The rector in question was the Revd Peter Wood, of whom John Mackoull has nothing but good to say:

> His character is truly apostolical; he is not only *revered* and *loved* by the inhabitants of *Broadwater* and *Worthing*, but by the whole county of Sussex; there is a *pleasing meekness* in his demeanour, with a face *illumined* with *benignity*. His heart glowing with piety, he is continually going about doing good. He possesses neither *pride* nor *avarice*. The parsonage house is called the Temple of Charity, *hospitality* stands at its gate, and invites the stranger and needy to refreshment.[10]

Revd Wood's church, however, was less to be admired than its rector. G., the anonymous author of *A Tour to Worthing*, tells us that in 1805 St Mary's, Broadwater was 'in the most deplorable condition, extremely old'. He adds that the church's appearance suggests that it has never been refurbished since it was built, since 'the outside bears severe marks of antiquity and decay, and the interior parts are nearly demolished … the whole is in a dreadful state of dilapidation'.

Broadwater's dilapidated church was a walk of just over a mile and a quarter from Stanford's Cottage, and there were two possible routes the Austen ladies could have taken. One was the main road, which, as it approaches Broadwater, runs just west of the manor house, which stands three hundred yards to the south of the church. The other was a footpath that passed two hundred and fifty yards to the east of the manor house. The route of the old footpath to Broadwater can still be walked. It starts just south of the railway line, at the northern end of Dagmar Street, and runs in a straight line northwards, following Beaumont Road as it approaches Broadwater. In Jane Austen's time the footpath ran through fields, with the Broadwater Brook less than half a mile to the east.

The other witness signature on the affidavit signed on 4 November was that of Fanny's mother, who had briefly returned to Worthing. This was almost certainly to collect Fanny's governess, Miss Sharpe, who, as we have seen, had not left the town at the same time as Fanny and her parents. Corroboration of this theory is provided by Fanny's diary, which records that on Friday 1 November she received a letter from Miss Sharpe 'to say she was coming home'.

Curiously, however, Fanny's diary does not record either her mother's absence from Godmersham or Miss Sharpe's return. Elizabeth Austen's trip to Worthing cannot have involved her being away from Godmersham for more than two nights, since on the Sunday Fanny writes that she 'breakfasted with Mama' and on the Tuesday she notes that her mother that day received a letter from her brother Edward, who was away at school. Therefore Elizabeth was clearly at Godmersham on the morning of 3 November and was back there at some point on 5 November.

There is no further record of the Austen ladies' movements for the rest of the year, so they may have spent Christmas at Stanford's Cottage. They were certainly not with Edward at Godmersham over the Christmas period, nor with James at Steventon rectory. We know, however, that Jane and Martha arrived at Steventon on Friday 3 January 1806, so if they did remain in

Worthing until the start of 1806, they presumably left the town on 2 January. For some reason it was not until a week later that Mrs Austen and Cassandra joined them at Steventon.[11]

If the Austen party was indeed still in Worthing over Christmas and New Year, it is pleasant to speculate that they may have been entertained at some point by 'sweet Mr Ogle' – whose wine-cellar at Warwick House was, as we saw in Chapter 2, so ample that careful provisions for dividing it up between his wife and his brother were made in his will.

Meanwhile, back at Godmersham, Fanny Austen had had a heavy cold over Christmas, but was better by 29 December; and on 1 January she set down in her diary her hopes for 1806: 'Heaven grant that this year may be happier & better spent than the last!'

Godmersham Park, Kent
This was the house that Fanny Austen's father, Edward, inherited from his adoptive father, Thomas Knight. Thomas's widow Catherine had a life-interest in Godmersham, but in 1797, three years after her husband's death, she vacated the house and signed it over to Edward. Fanny grew up at Godmersham and lived there until she married in 1820. The engraving comes from Edward Hasted's *The History and Topographical Survey of the County of Kent* (1799).

Chapter 4
Worthing in 1805

In the year 1805 Worthing, where Jane Austen spent between seven and twelve weeks from mid-September onwards, was still small, though growing quickly. The 1801 census gives the population of the parish of Broadwater as 1,018 and the census of 1811 records 2,692. Although Worthing was administratively separate by 1811, it was still part of Broadwater parish for census purposes, and by that date most of the total was accounted for by Worthing rather than Broadwater.[1] For the year 1805 – a date closer to the earlier census than the later – we may therefore extrapolate a population for Worthing alone of between 1,500 and 1,750.

The popularity of new resorts such as Worthing in the late eighteenth and early nineteenth centuries was largely a consequence of the war with France, which meant that the rich and well-born could no longer travel to Europe as they had done previously. Holidays at the English seaside became a substitute.

But even in tranquil Sussex it was impossible to forget about the hostile French. On 18 August 1805 – exactly a month before Jane Austen arrived in Worthing – a local newspaper reported that there had been an invasion scare the previous night:

> About eleven o'clock last night the whole of the inhabitants of this place were greatly alarmed by a fire which happened at Broadwater, about a mile from the town; by some accident a rack of furse was set on fire, which communicated to several others of the same quality, but of greater magnitude; the dryness of the furse, which was intended for the burning of bricks, made such a blaze that most of the inhabitants actually thought the French were landed, and were burning down the town; while others, not so frightened, hastened to the spot where the supposed enemy had landed, but soon discovered their mistake, and quietly returned back to bed.[2]

While somewhat comical, this episode shows how jittery people on the south coast were at this time – and indeed not all the threats posed by the French were imaginary. Eight days later the same newspaper reported an event which brought hostilities very close to Worthing. The report began with a brief summary of what happened: 'A privateer of no common magnitude was taken by one of our gun-brigs, near this part of the Channel last night, and safely conveyed into the port of Worthing this morning.' The 'port of Worthing' was Littlehampton, as is clear from the fuller account that followed:

> A French privateer secreted herself last night near Worthing, and, about four in the morning, captured a sloop, laden with sugars, teas, &c. &c., to the value of 7000l. As some part of the inhabitants were stirring at this early hour, they gave the alarm, and Captain Remus, in a revenue cutter, recaptured the sloop about five; and, after bringing her into Shoreham harbour,

went in pursuit of the privateer, which she captured in three hours after (a few shots being fired from the cutter), and brought her safe into Little Hampton.[3]

Princess Amelia, the youngest daughter of George III, had stayed in Worthing in the summer of 1798, but this royal visit did not have as great an impact as had been hoped.[4] The main reason for this was that Worthing's infrastructure and facilities were inadequate. Only in 1803 was proper drainage installed. In 1805 there was no market, no church, no theatre and no hotel. In addition, shopkeepers and tradesmen were still in short supply – in 1798 there had apparently been just two shopkeepers in Worthing, together with a carpenter and a brick-maker.[5]

Communications, too, were poor. The situation improved in 1804, when a new turnpike road was opened from West Grinstead via Washington to Worthing. Until then, Worthing had been approached by a series of winding country lanes. However, as we saw in Chapter 1, there was still no road east from the centre of the town in 1805, the only road into Worthing being from the north. In addition there was no promenade along the seafront. Buildings and gardens immediately abutted the shore. This remained the case until 1819–21, when the Esplanade was built between Greville Terrace (opposite Splash Point) and West Buildings, serving not only as a promenade but also, more importantly, as a sea defence.

It is of interest to note that in *A Picture of Worthing*, written after his visit in July 1804, John Evans refers six times to Worthing as a village – 'the other branches of the village'; 'throughout the village are many commodious houses', and so on – and only twice to it as a town. Curiously, one of the latter instances is in relation to an earlier period when Worthing was no more than a hamlet: 'Not many years ago it was an obscure fishing town, consisting of a few miserable huts.'

Henfrey Smail provides the following summary: 'We can visualise Worthing at this period of its history – i.e. the first decade of the nineteenth century – as a straggling village, still largely agricultural in character but rapidly outgrowing its former fishing village status and blossoming out as a thriving little seaside resort.'[6] Meanwhile G., the anonymous author of *A Tour to Worthing: Or, Idle Hours Not Idly Spent / Containing a Slight Sketch of the Country, Anecdotes, Etc.*, first published in 1805, writes: 'The town itself is only creating, therefore, offers little worthy of particular notice. Buildings are extending in every direction … [but] considerable time must necessarily elapse before any splendid arrangements can be carried into execution.'[7]

While Smail's and G.'s summaries give us a fair picture of Worthing as it was in 1805, the little town was developing so quickly that its character changed almost from one year to the next. In 1803 a lady visitor had written to a friend 'the people of Worthing are going building mad', and by the 1813 edition of *A Sketch of Worthing* John Mackoull is able to claim: 'We now present Worthing to our readers as one of the most fashionable and well attended watering-places in the kingdom.'

There is interesting material about Worthing as it was in the summer of 1805 in the reports of an unnamed daily newspaper (probably published in Brighton), which are reprinted verbatim in John Docwra Parry's 1833 book, *An Historical and Descriptive Account of the Coast of Sussex*. It should, however, be borne in mind that these pieces were clearly the work of the paper's Worthing correspondent, who is keen to stress what a fashionable little resort the town had become – as in this report of 16 August 1805:

This place, which has so much increased within these few years, particularly since Princess Amelia bathed here, with elegant and first-rate houses, is now so full that families retire to Brighton for want of room … Within these three years there have been no less than six streets built here, and at present occupied by persons of the first-rate fashion and fortune in England.[8]

Sea House Inn

In 1805 the Sea House Inn, which was probably built in the 1770s, was the largest inn in Worthing. It was replaced in 1826 by a much larger building, successively known as the Sea House Hotel, the Royal Sea House Hotel and the Royal Hotel, which was Worthing's leading hotel until it was destroyed by fire in 1901. Today the Arcade occupies the site. This watercolour by John Nixon dates from between 1805 and 1810.

Montague Place

This 1807 watercolour by Jacob Spornberg (1768–1840) of the view towards Montague Terrace from the north-east is of interest partly because it shows how much of central Worthing still consisted of unbuilt land in the early nineteenth century.

Stanford's Cottage

No contemporary pictures exist of Stanford's Cottage, where Jane Austen's party stayed in 1805. This 1963 photograph shows the cottage during the long period – encompassing most of the twentieth century – when it was used as a store-house for a furniture shop that stood in front of it at 20–22 Warwick Street. In Jane Austen's time these south-facing bow windows had an uninterrupted view towards the sea.

Bedford House and Stanford's Cottage

This photograph of 1907 shows how close Bedford House – known in the early nineteenth century as Lane's House – was to Stanford's Cottage. The buildings in the background were not present in 1805.

These 'six streets', which were in effect terraces rather than complete streets in the modern sense, are named as Montague Place (in fact built in the 1790s, and still standing today); Bedford Row (still standing); Copping's Row (a terrace on the west side of Marine Place, which was long ago swallowed up by extensions to the backs of the shops on the east side of South Street); Brook Street (later South Place, a short street connecting South Street and Ann Street, just to the east of where the old Town Hall later stood); and Beach Row and Hertford Street (neither of which are identifiable – modern-day Hertford Road is much later).[9]

Contemporary guide-books are no more objective than the reports of local newspapers, since they were generally written with the aim of promoting the town. As we saw in Chapter 1, Edward Ogle probably provided some of the material for John Evans's *A Picture of Worthing* – indeed John Mackoull seems to have thought that Ogle had written the book himself (see page 90) – and part of the book's purpose was to give the town a higher profile.

To this end, Evans reminds his readers of Princess Amelia's visit – by then seven years in the past – and adds:

> *Lord and Lady Melville*, together with the *Hon. Henry Addington* and his *Lady*, are to be ranked among [Worthing's] most recent visitors. Many noblemen and gentlemen with their families reside here during the summer months; and it is presumed that it will rival its opulent neighbour, Brighton, in retaining its visitors throughout the winter, when the draining and paving of the place are once completed.[10]

It is optimistic to suggest that Worthing – however well-drained and well-paved – would ever rival Brighton, even in the winter. However Evans's attempt to establish that Worthing was becoming an attractive destination for the well-born is not groundless. The visit of the Addingtons and the Melvilles is not documented elsewhere, so perhaps they were just passing through; but nonetheless they were major figures – Addington was Prime Minister in 1801–4 and Melville was First Lord of the Admiralty in 1804–6.

Stanford's Cottage, where Jane Austen stayed in 1805 – it is now a pizza restaurant – was the middle of three houses set back from the south side of Warwick Street, towards the eastern end. Next to it to the west was Lane's House, later known as Bedford House, which was demolished in 1940;[11] to its east was Lamport's Cottage, referred to in 1938 as having recently been demolished.[12] Just to the north of Lamport's Cottage there was another building, probably a pair of small houses. Lane's House, Stanford's Cottage and Lamport's Cottage all had open views towards the sea across a piece of ground known as Paine's Field. Between Lamport's Cottage and Stanford's Cottage a footpath ran from Warwick Street to the shore. About 1809 the building that comprised Stafford's Marine Library and Rebecca House was built at the sea-end of this footpath, which thereafter became known as Library Passage. (The northern end of this passage is still clearly defined, but the southern section now runs through the open space of the bus depot.)

Stanford's Cottage was named after its owner, Edward Stanford, who was a tailor, hatter and dealer in pianos. The possessive approach to the naming of property was common in Worthing (and elsewhere) in the early nineteenth century – as we have seen, the houses either side were called Lane's House and Lamport's Cottage – and in 1805 the name in use was Stanford's Cottage rather than Stanford Cottage. There is evidence for this in the letter (see pages 7–8) that establishes where in Worthing the Austen party stayed, in which Fanny Austen refers to the address to write to as 'Mr Stanfords'. In addition, the detailed street plan of Worthing that appears in all three editions of Wallis's *Stranger in Worthing, or New Guide to that Delightful Watering Place* (1826, 1832 and 1843) has the building marked as 'Stanfords Cottage'; and Stanford's Cottage is the name used by Edward Snewin, writing in 1899 about the Worthing he knew as a child in the 1820s.[13]

The variant form 'Stanford Cottage' seems to have come into use around the middle of the nineteenth century – it appears in post office directories of that period[14] – but it was never universally adopted, and Worthing's historians almost always refer to 'Stanford's Cottage'. Later the house lost its name altogether. It was not lived in after 1906, and by 1919 it had no address at all. For most of the twentieth century it was simply an unnamed store-house behind the premises of Colin Moore, 'Complete House Furnisher', at 20–22 Warwick Street. When the house was given its Grade II listing in October 1949, the listing text stated: 'It was originally called Stanfords Cottage but it is now only called a store-house.'

In 1805 Stanford's Cottage was a charming, bright house in an open setting, with views of the sea from the bow windows on its south side. On the Warwick Street side there was a paved courtyard with a pair of gates and an old chestnut tree in the middle.[15] The north side of Warwick Street opposite the cottage was not yet built, the houses there being erected only in 1807–8 on fields that had been part of the Warwick House estate until Edward Ogle sold them in 1807.[16] The fact that this was still open ground in Jane Austen's time is confirmed by the 1804 print of Warwick House and the Colonnade (reproduced on page 15), the left edge of which shows no continuation of the terrace – the 1814 version being amended to show that the row of buildings continued. Just to the north, Ann Street had recently been created, but was not yet built upon. The outlook from the north frontage of Stanford's Cottage was therefore over fields and a few scattered buildings towards Middle Street (subsequently West Street, and today North Street), with the downs beyond. On the right-hand side of this view were various old houses and cottages along the High Street as it ran north from the Colonnade. The area to the east and south-east of the row of four houses in which Stanford's Cottage stood was entirely open ground, since, as we shall see in Chapter 6, construction of Steyne Row (as the Steyne houses were originally known) and the Steyne Hotel had not yet begun.

Among the notable buildings within a few minutes' walk of Stanford's Cottage – all had been built within the previous dozen years – were the terrace of seven houses on the west side of Montague Place at the sea-end (c. 1794); Bath Buildings (built by 1800, now part of Bath Place), which at that time faced Montague Place across an open lawn; the three lodging-houses on the seafront known as Little Terrace (built soon after 1794) and the two known as Great Terrace (built by 1804); and Bedford Row (built by 1804).[17] All were built as lodging-houses – and, remarkably, all still survive, albeit some of them somewhat altered. (In Bath Place, houses 1–3 have been replaced by nondescript modern buildings and only one of the old houses still has its original curved bow windows.)

In 1805, unlike today, these buildings were not part of a dense, fully built environment. Some stood quite apart from other structures; others were among small clusters of buildings. Everywhere in central Worthing there were wide expanses of unbuilt land, lawns and fields. There were buildings on the east side of South Street, but on the west side was a meadow grazed by sheep and cows. The lower picture on page 89 shows the street as Jane Austen knew it.

Between Montague Place and the field that was later to become Steyne Gardens the seafront seems to have consisted – this takes some imagining – of just seven buildings spread along 450 yards. These were, from west to east: Wicks's Baths; the Sea House Inn; the New Inn; Marine Cottage (in 1816 this was enlarged to become the Wellington Inn, renamed the Pier Hotel in 1863); Great Terrace (two houses); Little Terrace (three houses); and an old inn which was replaced in 1807 by the Steyne Hotel. Of these buildings only Great and Little Terrace still stand, just to the west of the Dome.

...

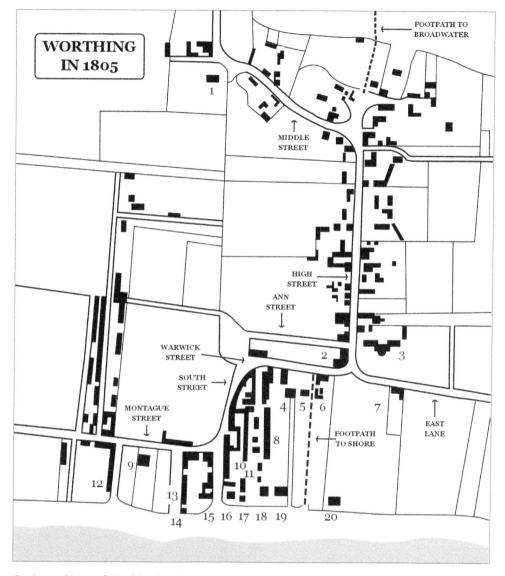

Conjectural Map of Worthing in 1805

1. Worthing House
2. The Colonnade
3. Warwick House
4. Lane's House
5. Stanford's Cottage
6. Lamport's Cottage
7. Badger's Buildings
8. Bedford Row
9. Sumner Lodge
10. Copping's Row
11. Stafford's Library
12. Montague Terrace
13. Bath Buildings
14. Wicks's Baths
15. Sea House Inn
16. New Inn
17. Marine Cottage
18. Great Terrace
19. Little Terrace
20. Inn (name unknown)

This map is based on a map printed in the 1814 edition of John Evans's *A Picture of Worthing* (a version of which is reproduced on page 74), with the buildings known not to have been present in 1805 removed. Inevitably there are areas of uncertainty, and in particular it is difficult to be sure how much of the area north of Montague Street was already built in 1805.

Worthing Seafront in 1810

The buildings in this early view of the seafront are, from the right of the mast of the sailing-boat: the Sea House Inn, the New Inn, Marine Cottage, Great Terrace, Little Terrace, Bedford Row, and the building that comprised Stafford's Marine Library and Rebecca House. This last building, the only one that was not present in 1805, was built between 1808 and 1810.

Great Terrace, Little Terrace and Stafford's Library in 1810

In the centre of the picture are Great Terrace and Little Terrace. To their right, just behind the small tree, is the southern end of Bedford Row. At the right of the picture are Stafford's Marine Library and, greyer in colour, Rebecca House. All these buildings still stand, although all that is left of the Stafford's Library / Rebecca House building is a single storey.

We will now consider what this small, scattered resort-town offered in the way of recreational activities for visitors such as the Austens. Since well-bred ladies would not have ventured into the town's inns, the main locations for social interaction were the town's two libraries, Spooner's in the Colonnade, almost opposite Stanford's Cottage, and Stafford's Marine Library, which in 1805 was in Marine Place, at that time the name of a small group of buildings just behind Marine Cottage.[18]

The primary function of libraries was of course the borrowing of books, and, writing in *A Picture of Worthing*, John Evans, 'aware of the usual trash of circulating libraries', is 'pleasingly disappointed in finding so many volumes worthy of attention'. Paul Potion, whose verse is often closely imitative of what Evans says in prose, makes the same point:

> In these sad novel-reading times,
> The writer of these humble rhymes
> Was pleasingly surpris'd to find
> The books were of a superior kind.

At the start of Chapter 8 of *Sanditon* Sir Edward Denham refers to the cheaper type of novel in almost identical terms to Evans:

> I am no indiscriminate Novel-Reader. The mere Trash of the common Circulating Library, I hold in the highest contempt. You will never hear me advocating those puerile Emanations which detail nothing but discordant Principles incapable of Amalgamation, or those vapid tissues of ordinary Occurrences from which no useful Deductions can be drawn.

This is one piece of evidence (there is another on pages 59–60) that Jane Austen knew Evans's book, and probably had it to hand when she was writing *Sanditon*. Indeed it would be surprising if during their stay in Worthing the Austen ladies did not acquire a copy of the principal guide-book to the town, whose first edition had been published earlier the same year.

Both libraries also kept copies of the most popular London newspapers, which Evans describes as 'a convenience that imparts a zest to the gratifications of retirement'.

The raffles referred to in Fanny Austen's diary entries for 19 and 20 September were among the entertainments offered by the libraries. We know that this is where they were held because G. tells us in *A Tour to Worthing* that a 'rivalship' has developed between the town's two libraries, and that at one of them 'public auctions of toys, trinkets, millinery, &c. have been substituted for raffles'. G. says that 'the humorous sallies and ingenious panegyrics of the Knight of the Hammer' make these auctions a favourite with both sexes, but unfortunately he does not tell us which of the town's two libraries stuck with raffles, and which replaced them with auctions.

On a more practical level, Stafford's Library served as Worthing's post office at the time of Jane Austen's visit, as John Evans tells us: 'Here is the *Post-Office*, for a boy passes and re-passes every day to Shoreham with letters; coming in about *eleven* in the morning, and going out at *three* in the afternoon.' By 1814, however, the Post Office had moved to Spooner's Library, since in the edition of his book published in that year Evans writes:

> At this Colonnade Library the Post Office is kept, and letters are delivered at eight o'clock in the morning, and dispatched thence at seven in the evening every day. A mail also passes through this town every day which conveys letters along the coast eastward and westward.

The relocation of the post office probably happened at the same time as Stafford's Library moved, in about 1809, from Marine Place to the new building on the seafront that it thereafter shared with Rebecca House. Perhaps Stafford preferred to use all the available space in his new premises for library-related activities. Or perhaps it was Edward Ogle that engineered the post office's move to the Colonnade Library, where it was not only more central (and convenient to Warwick House) but also in a building he owned.

Stafford's Library served another practical function at the start of the nineteenth century. We learn from an announcement in the *Morning Chronicle* of 13 September 1806 that every morning at seven o'clock 'accommodation coaches' set off from the Nelson Inn and the New Inn, arriving in London at five o'clock in the afternoon – and that Stafford's Library was the location where 'places and parcels' could be booked.

Even more important to a seaside town than the presence of libraries was of course the availability of bathing, and Evans tells us that those that chose to bathe in the sea were able to make use of bathing machines, of which there were about thirty at Worthing in 1805. The price for hiring one of these was a shilling, or sixpence for children under the age of seven. 'Proper persons' were in attendance, and Evans says that these attendants could be 'recommended for their civility'. Potion adds that the male and female machines were on separate parts of the beach, allowing 'the timid virgin' to 'kiss the blue translucent wave / At distance from th' intruding eye.'

The bathing machine experience was in fact rather unpleasant. They were often stuffy and smelly and, though most had small windows, were ill-lit. They were usually pulled into the water by horses – this was quite a rough ride – after which the occupant was able to take a sea-dip close to the machine, where he or she was invisible from the beach.

The view that bathing was beneficial was not universal. John Mackoull, for example, is sceptical, and the 1813 edition of *A Sketch of Worthing* includes the following warning:

> People are apt to imagine that the simple element of water can do no hurt, and that they may plunge into it at any time with impunity. In this, however, they are much mistaken; apoplexies have been known to have taken place by going into the cold bath – fevers excited by staying too long in it, and other maladies so much aggravated by its continued use, as to become absolutely incurable … It would therefore be well to consult some medical gentleman previous to making use of the bath, or immerging into the sea.

G. also has reservations about sea-bathing, but these are specific to Worthing:

> Worthing is yet in its infancy, consequently we cannot expect to find there perfection, but in the course of a few seasons, I trust, some better regulations will be adopted in respect to bathing; the present practice of ladies and gentlemen going in, sometimes nearly in the same place, and always at a distance sufficiently short, to distinguish each others features, being perfectly indecent and inconsistent with the rules of propriety and morality. I should also recommend to the gentlemen, to recollect the delicacy that is due to the female sex, and instead of lounging upon the beach, and indulging in unpleasant observations, to direct their attention to amusements more manly and becoming.

There was an alternative for those that found the prospect of sea-bathing too bracing – or too compromising – and Evans informs us of it: 'There is also a *warm bath*, belonging to *Mr John Wickes* [in fact Wicks]; it has been lately erected and is heated to whatever temperature may be required.' As we know from Fanny Austen's diaries, Cassandra took advantage of this facility on 20 September 1805.

For those tempted by more adventurous activities, Evans's book has a helpful section entitled 'Aquatic Excursions':

Here are *Pleasure Boats*, in which, for a few shillings, you may be wafted along the coast in safety. At the distance of three or four miles on the sea, WORTHING appears to advantage; its new buildings glisten on the eye – whilst backed by a wooded and variegated country, the imagination is at once delighted and refreshed ... These *Excursions on the water* are both healthy and pleasant. They recommend themselves by a fascinating variety; and after the example recently set by his Majesty at Weymouth – they will not be deemed a *vulgar* recreation, even by a fashionable world.

It is hard to believe that Jane, Cassandra and Martha – although perhaps not Mrs Austen – did not take advantage of the opportunity to take an aquatic excursion. As already indicated, they almost certainly had a copy of Evans's book, and Jane Austen would have been amused to be reassured that aquatic excursions were not vulgar recreations.

But then Worthing was in general a quiet and respectable little place. We know from John Mackoull that as late as 1813 there was still no policeman in the town:

> The inhabitants of Worthing judging the *purity* of other persons conduct from their own, do not conceive it necessary to have a peace officer in the place; as a proof of our assertion, the present constable of the *parish* resides *two miles* from Worthing. Therefore, those who may feel inclined to break the peace have nothing to fear from an *immediate* arrest. We trust our observations will have the effect of shewing the folly in thus subjecting the place and visitors to insult.

Meanwhile G., writing in 1805, informs us that 'neither routs [riotous revelries], balls, gaming, drinking, racing, cock-fighting, nor bustle are to be found at Worthing' and that the town is not a suitable destination for those 'whose entertainment consists, in indulging the vanity of parade and dress; in attending the levee's [*sic*] of the great and proud; in mixing in the assemblies of dissipation and vice; or in emptying bumpers [full glasses of wine] at the orgies of Bacchus'. Rather, Worthing offered the 'more rational amusements of riding, walking, sailing, fishing, or the field sports'.

As mentioned earlier in this chapter, there are interesting accounts of Worthing in 1805 in the reports of a daily newspaper of the time. The issue of 16 August 1805, for example, includes this straightforward description of the beach at Worthing and some of the activities enjoyed there:

> The beach, without a cliff, at low water extends six miles, and at ebb-tide, near three quarters, and is generally five hours' ebb, by which the ladies and gentlemen take delightful rides and walks, and in other parts it is occupied by some of the best cricket players in England, the sands being so fine and level.

A report of 19 August again fills the beach with activity, and indeed from an early hour:

> From the fineness of the morning yesterday, as early as six o'clock, the sands were crowded with fashionable families. After breakfast the beach and sands were crowded with barouches [four-wheeled horse-drawn carriages], curricles [open two-wheeled carriages], ponies, and donkeys.

Other pieces in the same newspaper contradict G's assurance that there was no gaming or racing in Worthing, although it is true that these races involved ponies and donkeys rather than thoroughbred horses. On 18 August 1805 the paper reports that 'last night pony and donkey racing were frequent on the sands', and on 28 August that the previous day 'the whole of the fashionable visitors' to the town had congregated on the sands to watch a two-mile pony race. There were four ponies involved, Lady Gordon's pony being the 2-1 favourite, but Mr Broderick's bay pony won by a length.[19]

In spite of excitements such as these, Jane Austen's stay in Worthing was probably a fairly low-key affair – less busy and demanding than being at Godmersham, with its round of regular activities, and various children in attendance even when Edward Austen's older sons were away at school. It is unlikely that the Austen party had much to do with the fashionable visitors who came and went, but doubtless they got to know some of the townsfolk. Perhaps they continued to see Elizabeth Austen's friends the Johnsons and Miss Fielding, and through them met other convivial people; and there was the regular social activity at the town's libraries. In addition, they were almost certainly entertained by Edward and Ann Ogle. In the late summer this would have been at the house the Ogles apparently occupied in Bedford Row during the season, but once the season was over the Ogles would have received their guests at Warwick House.

By the middle of October there would have been few visitors left in the town, which would have become rather dull and quiet – although quietness would have been a relative term in any town of the period, even a small one like Worthing. The bustle of the streets, the yelling of coster-mongers and the clatter of horses and carriages would have made for a cacophonous mixture. In addition, in the case of Worthing in 1805, there would have been much noise from all the building work that was going on.

Jane Austen would not have minded that Worthing was something of a backwater compared to London, Bath, or Brighton. She enjoyed walking, and would certainly have explored the countryside around Worthing on foot. This might sometimes have been quite challenging as autumn turned to winter, with many of the tracks becoming muddy and rutted. However for those not easily daunted there were numerous places of interest in the locality.

Furthest afield were the Iron Age hill forts of Chanctonbury and Cissbury, visits to which would probably have involved the hire of a pony and trap. An elevated location nearer Worthing – and within walking distance for a fit young woman – was Highdown Hill, where the miller and smuggler John Olliver built his own tomb twenty-seven years before his death in 1793, possibly partly as a hiding-place for contraband. In the 1813 edition of *A Sketch of Worthing* John Mackoull refers to a 'rural alcove' there which was popular with visitors:

> The alcove is about ten yards from the tomb; in this retreat the miller spent most of his leisure hours. It is also an agreeable resting-place for those who walk hither, and a very convenient tea-drinking box, many persons using it for that purpose, taking with them their tea and sugar only – during the season a person always is in attendance from the miller's house to supply the company with hot water, bread and butter, and every necessary article for the tea-table, an accommodation extremely agreeable and acceptable to many.

(Tea and, to some extent, sugar were expensive luxuries, so people brought their own.)

Other nearby attractions included the eccentric splendours of still-unfinished Castle Goring, built by the grandfather of the poet Shelley; High Salvington, with its beautiful views and its old mill; the cottage at Salvington where the jurist John Selden had supposedly been born in 1584, although the cottage seems actually to have dated from 1601;[20] Tarring, with its fifteenth-century houses and ancient fig gardens; and the village of Broadwater, with the historic estates of Broadwater Manor and Offington nearby.

As we shall see in the next chapter, some of these destinations provided Jane Austen with ideas for locations that were later to appear in *Sanditon*.

The Miller's Tomb

This tomb on Highdown Hill, which signally failed to impress Horace Smith's narrator in 1822 (see page 111), was built by the eccentric miller-cum-poet John Olliver twenty-seven years before his death. Already a tourist attraction in Jane Austen's time, Olliver's tomb still stands today, near the entrance to Highdown Gardens. The engraving above, with Olliver's mill just visible on the left, appeared in the 1813 and 1817 editions of John Mackoull's *A Sketch of Worthing*. The print below, showing the tomb seen from the miller's summer-house – which Mackoull describes as a 'very convenient tea-drinking box' – is by James Rouse of Fulham.

Selden's Cottage, Salvington
The cottage in this watercolour of 6 September 1834 was the supposed birthplace of John Selden (1584–1654), the great jurist, scholar and parliamentarian, described by the poet John Milton as 'the chief of learned men reputed in this land'. Originally called Lacies Cottage, it was demolished in the late 1950s after a serious fire. It was located about a mile and a quarter to the north-west of Stanford's Cottage, and, like the Miller's Tomb, was a regular destination for visitors to early Worthing.

The Old Palace, Tarring
Another early tourist destination was the village of Tarring, with its fifteenth-century houses and its famous fig gardens. There is a strong tradition linking Thomas à Becket with the village, and the building in this John Nixon watercolour of *c.* 1805–10 is often known as Thomas à Becket's Palace. However, although Archbishops of Canterbury travelling through Sussex in the early Middle Ages sometimes stayed in a previous building on the site, the earliest parts of this building (which still stands today) date back no further than the thirteenth century. In 1805 it was being used as a school.

Chapter 5

Worthing and Sanditon – The Parallels

Jane Austen was a novelist, not a travel-writer, and the town of Sanditon is not meant to be an exact replica of Worthing. Indeed Jane Austen muddies the coastal waters by giving her town a geographical position – between Eastbourne and Hastings – that implies Bexhill-on-Sea, over forty miles east of Worthing.[1] There is further camouflage in that Worthing appears in two other guises in her unfinished novel.

The first of these comes early in the first chapter, where Worthing is mentioned by its own name. Mr Heywood makes disparaging comments about seaside resorts, and Mr Parker responds that this criticism 'may apply to your large overgrown Places, like Brighton, or Worthing, or East Bourne – but not to a small Village like Sanditon'.[2] (By the time *Sanditon* was being written in 1817 Worthing could – just – be described as 'large and overgrown', but in 1805 it was itself little more than a village.)

The second 'alternative Worthing' in the book is another nascent resort, Brinshore. Mr Parker is vigorous in his denunciation of this rival, which he describes as in every way inferior to Sanditon (note that, while Sanditon's status as a 'small Village' is seen as desirable, Brinshore's being a 'paltry Hamlet' is to be despised):

> the attempts of two or three speculating People about Brinshore, this last Year, to raise that paltry Hamlet, lying, as it does between a stagnant marsh, a bleak Moor & the constant effluvia of a ridge of putrifying sea weed, can end in nothing but their own Disappointment. What in the name of Common Sense is to *recommend* Brinshore? – A most insalubrious Air – Roads proverbially detestable – Water Brackish beyond example, impossible to get a good dish of Tea within 3 miles of the place.

This looks very like a list of Worthing's less appealing characteristics at the time. The creation of the turnpike road in 1804 had far from solved all the town's road problems. Corroboration of the 'stagnant marsh' and 'insalubrious air' is provided by the fact that in the early nineteenth century the road that ran east to west at the northern entrance to the town (now called Teville Road) was known as Vapours Lane – a reference to the mists that were prevalent on the low-lying marshy land along the Teville Stream.[3] The author of *A Tour to Worthing / Or, Idle Hours Not Idly Spent* also refers to the problem of fog and damp, as well as that of seaweed:

> the town has nevertheless its disadvantages: the situation is low, consequently exposed to fogs and damps, and the effluvia arising from the sea weed, which is very improperly suffered to remain the whole season upon the shore, renders the town at particular periods very disagreeable.[4]

Another writer, albeit one with a vested interest – he was a doctor in Worthing at the time Jane Austen was there[5] – disputes the claim that the town had poor air quality. In his book, *A Topographical Description of Worthing / With Brief Notices of Places of Interest in the Vicinity / Usually Visited by Strangers / To Which is Prefixed / A Concise Essay / On Warm and Cold Bathing*, John Shearsmith attributes the allegation to envious rivals:

> it is well known that some of the attempts to undervalue its growing prosperity have had their foundation in the envy of interested individuals in rival situations on the same coast. By some of these would-be censors of the place, the air has been pronounced to be bad in the extreme! its situation low and marshy (the reverse being actually the case); that it is unsafe for any person, and more especially invalids, to remain beyond a certain period of the autumnal quarter.[6]

The approach taken by the 'interested individuals' to whom Shearsmith refers is so close to Mr Parker's that one wonders whether Shearsmith and Jane Austen both had in front of them a book or article in which some 'would-be censor' had attacked Worthing.

In creating the resort of Brinshore, Jane Austen seems to have been amusing herself by taking the aspects of Worthing that visitors found displeasing – in truth, they were few in number – and parcelling them up into a 'bad Worthing'. With the stagnant marsh and the putrefying seaweed out of the picture, she was then able to present her readers with a resort that offered only Worthing's more attractive qualities.

However the brief appearance in the first chapter of her novel of these two decoy Worthings in no way negates the identification of Worthing with Sanditon, and the points of resemblance between Sanditon and the Worthing of 1805 will now be dealt with in four sections.

First we will demonstrate the ways in which Warwick House and the area around it resembled Mr Parker's Trafalgar House and its hinterland. Next we will examine the parallels between Edward Ogle and Mr Parker, the eldest of the three brothers who were to have been at the heart of Jane Austen's novel. Then we will look at the resemblances between Broadwater and the village Mr Parker refers to in Chapter 4 as 'old Sanditon'. Finally we will discuss the influence on Sanditon House of Offington House and Broadwater Manor, the two historic estate houses that were located near Broadwater, and consider whether there may also have been a local inspiration for Denham Park.

...

The Battle of Trafalgar was fought on 21 October 1805, and Jane Austen was almost certainly still in Worthing when news of Nelson's victory reached England just over a fortnight later. Fanny Austen and her father, who had been back in Kent for six weeks, heard of it on 7 November. Her diary entry for that day, mixing the epic with the prosaic, reads as follows: 'Papa and I went to Canterbury. We heard of a very great Victory, we had obtained over the French, but that Lord Nelson was killed. I had a letter from Sophia Deedes.'

It may have been partly in reference to her time in the town that Jane Austen called Mr Parker's house Trafalgar House. Coincidentally, a real Trafalgar House was built in Worthing soon after her stay, on the seafront two hundred yards west of Montague Place. However Jane Austen probably never heard of it, and in any case it did not resemble Mr Parker's house either in its location or its character. (The real Trafalgar House was later the location of another royal visit to Worthing, when Princess Augusta – sister of Princess Amelia and of George IV – stayed there during the winter of 1829–30, after which it was renamed Augusta House in her honour. A modern block, also called Augusta House, now occupies the site.)

Worthing Sands, *c.* 1811

The building at the far right of this pen and wash representation of Worthing Beach is Greville (later Gravel) Terrace, which still stands today. To its left is the Steyne Hotel, with Steyne Row extending northwards, and beyond is the recently erected Stafford's Library / Rebecca House building. The unknown artist has unaccountably omitted Little Terrace from his picture, for the building depicted to the left of Stafford's Library is clearly Great Terrace.

Worthing Beach in 1808

This John Nixon watercolour of Worthing Beach is of interest not only for the animated nature of the scene but also for the comprehensive record of the seafront buildings as they were three years after Jane Austen's visit, the only addition since 1805 being the Steyne Hotel, built in 1807. At the centre of the picture in the distance can be glimpsed the signal-post at Heene (see also the illustration on page 58). At centre-right are Great Terrace and Little Terrace, with the newly built Steyne Hotel at far right. The fact that the Stafford's Library / Rebecca House building is not present provides proof that when Jane Austen stayed in Worthing in 1805 Stafford's Library was still located in Marine Place.

The Signal-Post at Heene
The naval signal-post at Heene was a link in the chain of intelligence from Beachy Head to Portsmouth. These signal-posts were situated at regular intervals along the coast, about four miles apart. There was another one at East Worthing, near the junction of today's A259 and B2223. This contemporary drawing also shows the low cliff that existed along part of the shore at Worthing in the early nineteenth century.

Worthing Beach in 1810
Prominent in this animated depiction of Worthing beach is the early oil street-lamp. The picture on page 37 shows that there were at least three of these on Worthing seafront by the 1820s.

There are several respects in which Sanditon's Trafalgar House closely matches Warwick House, not least its exposed situation. In Chapter 4 of *Sanditon*, Mr Parker says of his house: 'We have all the Grandeur of the Storm, with less real danger, because the Wind meeting with nothing to oppose or confine it around our House, simply rages & passes on.'

The situation of Warwick House was likewise exposed to wind and storm, with no buildings to the south between it and the sea, apart from a row of three small cottages known as Badger's Buildings – but these were too far from the house to have provided much of a windbreak. The land to the east was totally open terrain. In 1805 the only buildings to the south-west were the Colonnade and the small group of houses that included Stanford's Cottage, and an old inn on the seafront, on the site of which Edward Ogle was soon to build the Steyne Hotel. Only to the north was there a significant number of buildings – the houses and cottages along the High Street.

Jane Austen's detailed account of Trafalgar House in Chapter 4 of *Sanditon* offers a number of resemblances between it and Warwick House. She begins her description thus:

> Trafalgar House, on the most elevated spot on the Down was a light elegant Building, standing in a small Lawn with a very young plantation round it.

The illustrations on pages 15 and 16 demonstrate that Warwick House was, like Trafalgar House, 'a light, elegant building', and the 1890 plan of the house and grounds on page 21 shows the trees that would have been 'a young plantation' in Jane Austen's time. This young plantation reminds us, too, of Shearsmith's account of Ogle's having 'expended very considerable sums of money … in the formation of pleasure grounds, walks, and shrubberies'. John Evans also records that 'the lower part of the mansion [was] encircled with a shrubbery'.[7]

Jane Austen's description of Trafalgar House continues as follows:

> [It was] about an hundred yards from the brow of a steep, but not very lofty Cliff – and the nearest to it, of every Building, excepting one short row of smart-looking Houses, called the Terrace, with a broad walk in front, aspiring to be the Mall of the Place. In this row were the best Milliner's shop & the Library – a little detached from it, the Hotel and Billiard Room – Here began the Descent to the Beach, & to the Bathing Machines – & this was therefore the favourite spot for Beauty & Fashion. – At Trafalgar House, rising at a little distance behind the Terrace, the Travellers were safely set down.

Today we almost invariably think of a cliff as something high and precipitate, but in earlier times the word was often used of a feature that we would regard as little more than a steep slope. The shoreline at Worthing has changed considerably over the last two hundred years, and in Jane Austen's time there was indeed a low cliff at Heene, as is demonstrated by the contemporary drawing reproduced opposite (top). This image is taken from *The Worthing Map Story*, where Henfrey Smail's caption refers to the 'low cliff that formerly existed along the shore at Worthing'.

However there does not seem to have been a cliff, even in these modest terms, at Worthing itself, since John Evans tells us in *A Picture of Worthing*: 'The access to the sands is inviting, there being not the least cliff or sudden descent, by which the safety of even an infant may be endangered.' This description is confirmed by the various pictures in this book of the seafront between Montague Place and Steyne Gardens.

Jane Austen's 'short row of smart-looking Houses, called the Terrace, with a broad walk in front, aspiring to be the Mall of the Place' seems to have been taken directly from Evans's book, where this appears: 'A little row of houses on the edge of the beach, pleasantly situated, is denominated the Terrace; though the number of the houses is scarcely sufficient to merit that appellation.' Evans is referring to the five houses of Great Terrace and Little Terrace, which still stand on the seafront, three hundred yards to the south-west of where Warwick House stood. Jane Austen's 'short row' replicates Evans's 'small number of houses'.

Jane Austen situates Sanditon's (sole) library in 'the Terrace'. As we saw in Chapter 4, Stafford's Marine Library, one of the two libraries in Worthing in 1805, was at that time located just off the seafront in Marine Place, a few yards west of Great Terrace – a reasonably close, but not exact, match for the location of Sanditon's library.

Jane Austen also places Sanditon's hotel in this locality: it is 'a little detached' from 'the Terrace'. This suggests the Sea House Inn (see illustration on page 43), which was about sixty-five yards to the west of Great Terrace, just the other side of South Street. This was the town's largest inn in 1805. Indeed in the 1813 edition of *A Sketch of Worthing* it is referred to as the Sea House Hotel – although this was probably because John Mackoull was friends with the landlord, Mr Parsons, about whom he writes with particular enthusiasm. By the time of the publication of the 1817 edition of *A Sketch of Worthing*, Mr Parsons has been replaced by Mr Tuppen, and Mackoull refers to the establishment by its usual more modest title. The closeness of the hotel and 'the Terrace' in Sanditon is confirmed at the start of Chapter 9 of the novel, when Charlotte is ascending from 'the Sands to the Terrace' when she sees 'a Gentleman's Carriage with Post Horses standing at the door of the Hotel'.

Jane Austen's reference to the beach at Sanditon being 'the favourite spot for beauty and fashion' is also a match for Worthing, where the sands were the original promenade. Later, from around 1811, the Steyne became 'the fashionable promenade' and 'mustering point' for the town, before it was replaced in its turn by the Esplanade between Splash Point and West Buildings, which was completed in 1821.[8] At the time of Jane Austen's visit in 1805 there was no road or raised walk-way along the seafront, and indeed nothing to prevent the town flooding when tides were abnormally high.

There are a couple of other minor references in *Sanditon* which seem to echo early Worthing. One comes near the end of Chapter 4 when, as the party approaches the main part of Sanditon for the first time, 'a Prospect House, a Bellevue Cottage, & a Denham Place were to be looked at by Charlotte with the calmness of amused Curiosity'. Although not located at the entrance to the town, early Worthing had a Prospect Place and a Prospect Row – they were just off the seafront at the western edge of the town – and the northern part of Portland Road was known as Belle Vue.

Finally, a few sentences later, there is a reference to Charlotte's looking out from Trafalgar House over 'unfinished Buildings' – and there would have been many of these at the time of Jane Austen's stay at the height of the town's building boom.

…

Jane Austen probably first encountered Edward Ogle at the library he owned in the Colonnade building, half-way between his house and Stanford's Cottage and less than a minute's walk from each. In 1805 the town's two libraries were the only establishments which offered entertainment in the evenings for respectable ladies, and we know that some of the Austen ladies went to one of the town's libraries on the Thursday and the Friday of the week that Fanny Austen was in Worthing.

The library in *Sanditon* is managed by Mrs Whitby, who, when Mr Parker takes the Heywoods there after dinner on the day of their arrival, is 'sitting in her inner room, reading one of her own Novels for want of Employment'. She then 'came forward without delay from her Literary recess, delighted to see Mr Parker again, whose manners recommended him to every body'. Jane Austen was almost certainly remembering Mrs Spooner, who ran Ogle's library in the Colonnade. In spite of the fact that the location of the library in Sanditon is a better match for Stafford's Library, it is likely that Spooner's was the establishment the Austen ladies generally patronised. This is not just because it was almost opposite Stanford's Cottage – Stafford's Library in Marine Place was only 250 yards away – but also because Ogle's new library would have been modern and well-appointed and, since it was managed by a woman, probably quieter and more respectable than Stafford's. Indeed Stafford's premises in Marine Place must have fallen some way short of the competition provided by the Colonnade Library, since, as we have seen, he relocated about four years later to a brand-new building directly on the seafront.

The library is our first link between Ogle and Mr Parker in *Sanditon*, for Mr Parker regularly went there to monitor new arrivals in the town: 'Mr P. could not be satisfied without an early visit to the Library, & the Library Subscription book.' When he and the Heywoods went there the first evening, the list was disappointing, being 'not only without Distinction, but less numerous than he had hoped'. This routine looks like something that Jane Austen remembered from Edward Ogle.

Likewise the account in Chapter 2 of Mr Parker's expatiating on the merits of Sanditon was almost certainly based on personal exposure to Ogle's effusions about the town that was his obsession:

> By such he was perceived to be an Enthusiast; – on the subject of Sanditon, a complete Enthusiast. – Sanditon, – the success of Sanditon as a small, fashionable Bathing Place was the object, for which he seemed to live. A very few years ago, & it had been a quiet Village of no pretensions; but some natural advantages in its position & some accidental circumstances having suggested to himself, & the other principal Land Holder, the probability of its' becoming a profitable Speculation, they had engaged in it, & planned & built, & praised & puffed, & raised it to Something of young Renown – and Mr. Parker could now think of very little besides. … He could talk of it for ever. – It had indeed the highest claims; – not only those of Birthplace, Property and Home; – it was his Mine, his Lottery, his Speculation & his Hobby Horse; his Occupation, his Hope & his Futurity.

This is a close match for Worthing in 1805 and for Edward Ogle's role in the town, and Mr Parker seems very similar in character to Ogle. Both were energetic speculators, developers and publicists, with an obsessive streak. We have no first-hand accounts of Ogle – other than from his enemy, John Mackoull – so we do not know how he came across to those who knew him; but the eccentricity that was part of Mr Parker's character was perhaps not a feature of Edward Ogle's.

Although it is by Mr Parker that Sanditon is dominated, Jane Austen creates a second individual involved in developing the town – Lady Denham – for whom there is no parallel in early nineteenth-century Worthing, since, as already indicated, most of the important building that took place in the town during this period was either on Ogle's land, or at his instigation, or both. However Lady Denham's activities in Sanditon seem to be less extensive than Mr Parker's, and indeed in Chapter 3 Mr Parker tells Charlotte Heywood, the novel's heroine, that he finds Lady Denham's approach too timid – she lacks his own vigorous, risk-taking entrepreneurial spirit:

> She … enters into the improvement of Sanditon with a spirit truly admirable – though now & then, a Littleness *will* appear. She cannot look forward quite as I would have her – & takes

alarm at a trifling present expence, without considering what returns it *will* make her in a year
or two. That is – we think *differently*, we now & then, see things *differently*, Miss H.

The circumstances of Mr Parker's background bear only a passing resemblance to Edward
Ogle's. In the first chapter of the book we learn that Sanditon had been Mr Parker's birthplace
and that he was 'by no means the first' of his family to hold landed property in the parish of
Sanditon. Edward Ogle, on the other hand, was an incomer.

  In the second chapter of *Sanditon* Jane Austen provides further information about Mr Parker's
family:

> The Facts ... he laid before them were that he was about 5 & 30 – had been married, – very
> happily married 7 years – & had four sweet children at home ... he was of a respectable family
> & easy though not large, fortune; – no Profession – succeeding as eldest son to the Property
> which 2 or 3 Generations had been holding & accumulating before him; – that he had 2 Brothers
> and 2 Sisters – all single & all independant – the eldest of the two former indeed, by collateral
> Inheritance, quite as well provided for as himself.

Edward Ogle had just one brother – although this brother was, as in the case of Mr Parker's next
brother, a rich man – and four sisters. He was some ten years older than Mr Parker, being about
forty-six in 1805. Unlike Mr Parker, Edward Ogle's wealth largely derived from trade, although
what we know of the Ogle brothers' background in the north of England suggests that they
came from a family that was already well off. And Edward Ogle had no children, which was no
doubt part of the reason he had so much energy to put into the development of Worthing.

  Edward's brother James was also involved to some extent in Edward's business activities in
Worthing, so he must have made intermittent visits to the town. Even if Jane Austen never met
James Ogle, she would – if she spent any time in Edward Ogle's company – have heard Edward
talk of him, in view of the brothers' closeness and their joint commercial interests. It is therefore
just possible that James Ogle, whom we earlier saw referred to as 'a gentleman held in much
estimation for his politeness and urbanity', provided partial inspiration for Mr Parker's middle
brother Sidney, who is described in Chapter 12 as 'about 7 or 8 & 20, very good-looking, with a
decided air of Ease & Fashion, and a lively countenance'. However the connection is slight. Also
Sidney Parker is twenty years younger than James Ogle, who was about forty-eight in 1805.

  But we would, in any case, not expect resemblances to be exact. Jane Austen was not writing
a biography of Edward Ogle. The outlines of Tom Parker, Trafalgar House and the town of
Sanditon were certainly sketched from life, but the application of the paint was guided by Jane
Austen's imagination. As with any writer of fiction, she needed to shape characters and places in
ways appropriate to her narrative and her themes. In addition she would have not have wanted
her sources of inspiration to be over-obvious.

...

In the fourth chapter of the novel, Mr Parker uses the term 'modern Sanditon' for the resort part
of Sanditon and 'old Sanditon' for the village located just to the north of it. The latter is first
referred to when Mr Parker, Charlotte and the others are driving south towards the coast:

> They were now approaching the Church & real village of Sanditon, which stood at the foot
> of the Hill they were afterwards to ascend – a Hill, whose side was covered with the woods
> & enclosures of Sanditon House and whose Height ended in an open Down where the new

Broadwater from the North

This James Rouse engraving of the approach to Broadwater from the north shows how prominent St Mary's Church was amongst the small cluster of humble village houses. On the right is the entrance to Offington Park.

Broadwater from the South

Another James Rouse engraving, this time showing Broadwater from the entrance to Worthing House, which stood on the low ridge between Broadwater and Worthing seafront. (Stoke Abbott Court occupies the site today.) The road running north through the centre of the picture is today's Chapel Road, the northern section of which was at that time known as North Street. Although this road appears on the 1814 map of Worthing (see page 74), it was not in fact completed till 1816. The road joining from the right is today's North Street, by that time West Street, and previously Middle Street. At the far right of the picture is the corner of the barn that was used for early theatrical performances before the Ann Street theatre was built in 1807.

Buildings might soon be looked for. A branch only, of the Valley, winding more obliquely towards the Sea, gave a passage to an inconsiderable Stream, & formed at its mouth, a 3rd Habitable Division, in a small cluster of Fisherman's Houses ... Not that [Mr Parker] had any personal concern in the success of the Village itself; for considering it as too remote from the Beach, he had done nothing there – but it was a most valuable proof of the increasing fashion of the place altogether. If the *Village* could attract, the Hill might be nearly full ... In ascending, they passed the Lodge-Gates of Sanditon House, & saw the top of the House itself among its Groves. It was the last Building of former Days in that line of the Parish.

The location and character of 'old Sanditon' – and its relationship to 'modern Sanditon' – are a close match for the village of Broadwater, a mile and a quarter north of Worthing seafront.

John Feltham, the author of *A Guide to All the Watering and Sea-Bathing Places for 1813*, is dismissive of Broadwater, which he says 'looks contemptible when contrasted with the growing splendour' of Worthing. However John Mackoull, writing in the edition of *A Sketch of Worthing* he published in the same year – while acknowledging that until recently Broadwater has been an unimpressive settlement – finds evidence of recent improvement: 'It is but a few years since that it had a most wretched and shabby appearance; it has now become, from a poor, mean, beggarly place, a delightful and rural village, containing many very pleasant houses.' In the 1817 edition of his book Mackoull explains the reason that the village has improved so much: 'Like most villages out of the common road, near the sea-side, it was formerly a very poor and comfortless spot' but, as the result of Worthing's having become a 'watering-place of celebrity', 'there is now a sufficiency to admire and be pleased with'.

This coheres with the account of Mr Parker's noting – although taking only a passing interest in – the evidence of a certain amount of tourist activity in old Sanditon.

The branch of the valley 'winding more obliquely towards the sea' from old Sanditon is matched in the geography of Broadwater, to the east of which there is a wide corridor of low-lying land curving in a south-east direction to the coast about a mile east of Worthing. As late as medieval times this had been a tidal inlet of the sea (indeed it was the 'broad water' that gave the village its name) and, as in the novel, an 'inconsiderable stream' – the Broadwater Brook – runs through this low-lying land to the sea.

Broadwater itself is, like old Sanditon, low-lying, a fact easily missed by a twenty-first-century visitor. On the modern Ordnance Survey map, triangulation points a few hundred yards to the north-east and south-west of Broadwater church show land that is, respectively, only thirteen and three metres above sea level. Also, although the slope up to it is very gentle, there is a low ridge at the northern approach to Worthing. That slope and ridge are, however, less substantial geographical features than the 'hill' leading up to an 'open down' which Jane Austen gives Sanditon.

The village of Broadwater would certainly have been well known to the Austen ladies since, with no church in Worthing, St Mary's, Broadwater is the church they would have attended on Sundays – for example on 22 September, when, as we saw in Chapter 3, Fanny Austen's diary records that some of the party (including 'Aunt Jane') went to church. And Jane Austen was also in Broadwater on 4 November, when she witnessed Martha Lloyd's affidavit in front of the rector.

...

While Tom Parker's Trafalgar House was certainly based on Warwick House, it is less easy to make a definite link between Lady Denham's Sanditon House and any one demesne in the locality.

However Jane Austen is most unlikely to have had in mind the somewhat presumptuously named Worthing House. Formerly known as Belvidere House and occupied by a schoolmaster called Tidey, the house had recently been renamed after being acquired by John Newland of Broadwater Manor, who had put in place 'considerable improvements'.[9] However, in spite of its grand name, Worthing House, which was located about half a mile from the sea at the northern extremity of the town (Stoke Abbott Court stands on the site today), was no more than – in Shearsmith's phrase – a 'very excellent family house', and about the same size as Lane's House, next to Stanford's Cottage. Worthing House served as a lodging-house for prosperous visitors, but it had little status in the town and its grounds were fairly modest.

The most likely candidates for Sanditon House, which Jane Austen tells us was situated near old Sanditon, are two substantial houses, part of centuries-old estates, which were located in or near the village of Broadwater. One, Broadwater Manor, now a school, is situated just to the east of today's A24 and about a mile north of Stanford's Cottage. The other, Offington House, which was demolished in 1963, stood a mile north-west of Broadwater Manor, set three hundred yards back from the London road in extensive parkland.

The two estates located close to Broadwater both had long histories. Offington, much the grander of the two, can be traced back to the ownership of Earl Godwin (father of King Harold) before the Norman conquest. An earlier house at Offington had been vast, with some sixty-eight rooms, but the handsome Georgian house that stood in Jane Austen's time dated from about 1780. The estate that became the manor of Broadwater was equally old, being recorded in 1066 as in the ownership of one Wigot of Wallingford. In 1805 the squire of Offington was William Margesson, High Sheriff of Sussex and an officer in the local corps of volunteers (also known as the County Yeomanry). Broadwater Manor was owned by John Newland, who was active in the town's affairs and, as one of the town commissioners, would certainly have known Edward Ogle well.

So which of Broadwater Manor and Offington House more closely resembles Sanditon House? Jane Austen does not have time to paint a detailed picture of the house itself, which we enter for the first time only on the last page of the unfinished novel. All we are told is that it was 'large & handsome' and that the sitting room was 'well-proportioned & well-furnished'.

However we know more about its location. In Chapter 4 of *Sanditon* we learn that Sanditon House was 'the last Building of former days' in old Sanditon as travellers from the north ascended towards the ridge where the first buildings of the modern resort of Sanditon were located. This is suggestive of Broadwater Manor rather than Offington House, which stood a mile north-west of the centre of the village. In addition we learn at the start of Chapter 3 that Lady Denham had inherited Sanditon House from her first husband, Mr Hollis, whose property included 'a large share of the Parish of Sanditon, with Manor and Mansion House' – in which respect Sanditon House is again a good match for Broadwater Manor.

In other ways, however, Offington appears the more likely inspiration. Broadwater Manor stands only about thirty yards from the London road, whereas Offington, like Sanditon House, was well set back. (The contemporary print reproduced on page 63 depicts the entrance to Offington, with Broadwater in the background.) Writing in 1824, Shearsmith describes Offington as follows:

> It is situated about a mile to the westward of Broadwater, the grounds, being skirted by the London road, from which there is a good view of the front of the house. The approach to it for pedestrians is across a small triangular tract of land called *Broadwater Green*, which abuts upon a part of the grounds denominated the Grove – a delightful avenue walk, about half a mile in extent, and much resorted to in summer for its verdant turf, and the shade it affords.

Broadwater Manor House

Broadwater Manor House is situated just to the east of the London road, three hundred yards south of the parish church of St Mary's, Broadwater. Today it is a preparatory school.

Offington House

This 1826 engraving of Offington House shows the view of the house seen by travellers proceeding towards Broadwater on their way to Worthing. The house was demolished in 1963, but most of the park had already been built over during the previous thirty-five years.

There are distinct echoes of this in Jane Austen's description of the approach to Sanditon House on the second-last page of *Sanditon*. From the road, the top of Sanditon House is just visible 'among its Groves' (Shearsmith used 'Grove'). There are two sets of gates, a quarter of a mile apart – one on the main road, and one at the entrance to the grounds – and between them 'a broad, handsome, planted approach, between fields'. Jane Austen also provides a specific detail that is strongly suggestive of Offington House, which, although it was approached by a long drive leading from the London road to the east, stood much closer to a second road on its west side (Offington Lane, now part of the A2031):

> These Entrance Gates [these were the second set of gates, near the house itself] were so much in a corner of the Grounds or Paddock, so near one of its Boundaries, that an outside fence was at first almost pressing on the road – till an angle *here*, & a curve *there* threw them to a better distance.

Another indicative point is that William Margesson, the squire of Offington, was famously hospitable to visitors, as John Mackoull tells us:

> Offington house still retains the old English custom of giving a welcome reception to all travellers; the poor and needy are always sure to meet with relief from the liberal-minded owner, whose strong October [beer] not unfrequently renders the guest somewhat troublesome. During the season at Worthing *Offington house* presents a continual scene of
> Rural life in all its joy
> And elegance, such as Arcadian song
> Transmits from ancient uncorrupted times.[10]

Jane Austen's first few weeks in Worthing were at the height of the season, so perhaps the Austen ladies were entertained at Offington, possibly having been introduced to Margesson by Edward Ogle. If not, they may have taken advantage of Offington's general welcome to travellers and visitors.

Interestingly, John Mackoull, while unstinting in his praise of its owner, does not think much of the house itself:

> Offington house has undergone much alteration, and at present makes but an indifferent appearance, being low and heavy, built of stone, and quite plain in front, with two small projecting wings. The ground which surrounds it, is inclosed with a rough wall, and has the appearance of a small park, with good groups of timber, but no deer.

Nonetheless the print of Offington House does not contradict Jane Austen's description of Sanditon House as large and handsome – Offington's size can be gauged from the fact that it had fourteen bedrooms on the first floor – and all the evidence points to its having served as the principal inspiration for Lady Denham's mansion.

One further important house is briefly mentioned in Jane Austen's novel – Denham Park, occupied by Lady Denham's nephew Sir Harry Denham. All that we know of it is that it was 'in the Neighbourhood of Sanditon' and that it was damp. This is not much to go on, but three houses come to mind as possible candidates.

Two were houses on historic estates located near the village of Findon, five miles north of Worthing. One of these was Muntham Court, two miles north of Findon and about half a mile west of the road from Worthing to London. Muntham Court had been owned since 1765 by a remarkable man called William Frankland, who had spent twenty years in Bengal working for the East India Company, and had later travelled extensively in Persia. In his later years he became something of a recluse, his time being 'principally directed to improvements in science, and the application of mechanics to manufacturing processes'. His house became virtually a museum, and he seems to have welcomed visitors, so it is possible that the Austen ladies went to see his exhibits. Frankland died on 28 December 1805, when Jane Austen may still have been in Worthing. The house was demolished in 1961, and Worthing's crematorium was built on the site of the old tennis courts.

The second candidate is Findon Place, about a quarter of a mile west of the old London road through the centre of Findon village, and just east of the parish church. The Findon Place estate had been acquired in 1787 by William Richardson, who died in 1801, and in 1805 his widow, Mary was living there. It was about this time that she had the house enlarged by the addition of a new east wing. Findon Place still stands today.

A third possibility is that Denham Park was suggested by Castle Goring, four miles north-west of Worthing. This splendid house was the eccentric project of Bysshe Shelley, grandfather of the poet. It is believed to be unique in Britain in having a castellated north front – its design inspired by nearby Arundel Castle – and a Palladian south front. Construction had started in the early 1790s, and, although the house was still not complete in 1805, it was already the object of much admiration. Jane Austen would certainly have seen it, either on a more than averagely hearty walk or while driving past on the Arundel road. The house still stands today, although the estate is now separate.

G. singles out Castle Goring for special mention in *A Tour to Worthing*, telling us that, although the normal route to Arundel was through Littlehampton, travellers frequently took the northerly route specifically 'in order to view an elegant residence erecting by Shelley, Esq.'. He says that £100,000 had already been spent on the house and that it was believed that another £50,000 would be needed to finish it. Although G. wonders what 'those interested in Mr Shelley's fortune may feel' about the expense, he considers 'the country under an obligation to him for this noble and magnificent monument of art and genius'.

There is minor point of similarity between Denham Park and Castle Goring in that both Harry Denham and Bysshe Shelley were baronets. Although Shelley did not yet have his title in 1805 – the baronetcy was created on 3 March 1806 – Jane Austen would almost certainly have been aware of the Shelley family's title by the time that she started writing *Sanditon* in 1817, two years after Sir Bysshe Shelley's death.

Muntham Court

Muntham Court stood two miles north of Findon, about half a mile west of the road from London to Worthing. The house was demolished in 1961, and Worthing's crematorium was built on the site of the old tennis courts.

Findon Place

The other great house near Findon was Findon Place, which still stands today, about a quarter of a mile west of the old London road through the centre of the village, and just east of the parish church of St John the Baptist.

Castle Goring
Castle Goring, built by Bysshe (later Sir Bysshe) Shelley, grandfather of the poet, is believed to be the only house in Britain with one castellated and one Palladian façade. The castellated façade, above, faces north, and the Palladian façade, below, is south-facing. Castle Goring survives, and after years of neglect was acquired in 2013 by a new owner and comprehensively restored. These engravings date from 1832.

Chapter 6

Edward Ogle and the Development of Worthing

In 1801, when Edward Ogle arrived in Worthing, there had been a fair amount of recent building activity, albeit somewhat haphazard in nature; and more was imminent. In the main this consisted of terraces of lodging-houses, and there was no coherent development plan, nor any attention to the town's facilities or infrastructure. Ogle's approach, however, was focused and methodical.

Threaded through this chapter – for which Ogle would not thank us – is the commentary of the egregious John Mackoull. We shall learn more about Mackoull's own life, and about his feud with Ogle, in Chapter 7. However it is impossible to keep this irrepressible figure out of an account of the development of early Worthing, since the most detailed and colourful – if idiosyncratic – picture of the town that Ogle built appears in the three editions (1811, 1813 and 1817) of Mackoull's book *A Sketch of Worthing*.

Ogle's first project, which he set in motion almost immediately upon acquiring the Warwick House estate, was to build the Colonnade (see illustrations on page 15) at the corner of Warwick Street and High Street and just across the road from his house. At the southern end of the building, which probably dates from about 1802, was the library run by Mary Spooner, while at the northern end there were three lodging-houses, approached by stone steps from the High Street. (The Colonnade was badly damaged by fire in 1888 and then restored in a more modest form, and the further 1936 reconstruction – this version still stands today – bears little resemblance to the fine building that Jane Austen knew.)

We have seen in previous chapters what important social institutions libraries were, so it is not surprising that Edward Ogle made a priority of building a terrace that included provision for one. Indeed the town's libraries seem to have engaged in fierce competition, and the next chapter will include an account of the acrimonious rivalry among the town's library-owners after John Mackoull opened his own establishment in about 1810.

Once the building of his library was under way, Ogle turned his attention to the desirability of Worthing's having a theatre. In the summer of 1802 – and seemingly in subsequent summers – the actor-manager Thomas Trotter held performances in a barn at the top of High Street. There was a three-month season, from August to October, with performances on Mondays, Wednesdays and Fridays. These productions were well received, and on 29 June the following year thirty-four residents signed a petition advocating the construction of a permanent theatre. The name at the head of the list, inevitably, was that of Edward Ogle. Edward Stanford, the owner of the cottage where Jane Austen stayed, was another of the signatories, as were Michael Morrah, the town's principal doctor, who was the Treasurer of the Board of Commissioners; Mary Spooner, of the Colonnade Library; and John Wicks, proprietor of the town's warm baths on the seafront.[1]

It was Ogle who financed the building of the theatre on land he owned on the north side of Ann Street. The theatre opened on 7 July 1807 with a – to our eyes rather incongruous – double bill of Shakespeare's *The Merchant of Venice* and a farce called *Children in the Wood*. Nine days later the comedy *The Honey Moon* and the farce *Of Age Tomorrow* were performed 'by desire of Mrs Ogle, to a fashionable audience'.[2] The first season was a great success, and on 4 February 1808 Ogle sold the theatre and the land adjoining it for £2,260 to Thomas Trotter. Ogle, ever the entrepreneur, had set in motion a project which contained an element of risk. Then, seeing it prosper, he took his profit, and moved on.[3]

On the playbill for the opening night, the theatre was referred to as 'New Theatre, Worthing', but it soon became just 'The Theatre'. Then, from 1813 or 1814 onwards, it was known as the Theatre Royal, which it remained for the rest of its relatively short existence. It closed in 1855 and the building became a warehouse for Worthing's main grocer, Potter, Bailey & Co. When the building was finally demolished in 1970, it had housed groceries for more than twice as long as it had entertained theatre-goers.

We need to break off briefly to say something about Thomas Trotter, who also contributed much to Worthing during the first quarter of the nineteenth century. Like Ogle he was a man of enormous energy and, again like Ogle, his activities were not confined to Worthing. He also ran theatres – often simultaneously – in Brighton, Shoreham, Littlehampton, Arundel, Gravesend, Hythe, Maidstone and Southend. But Worthing was the centre of his empire, and here his activities extended beyond the theatrical. It was he who, in about 1818, built the fine building on the seafront – demolished in 1940 – that comprised the Royal Baths and Marlborough House (see illustration on page 110). He was also the driving force behind the construction in 1819–21 of the Esplanade, the raised walkway between Splash Point and West Buildings.

Indeed by the time he died Trotter had a substantial property portfolio in Worthing. The list of his assets prepared for an auction held in 1852, a few months after his death in September 1851, included the Theatre Royal; the 'elegant cottage *ornée* [correctly, *orné*]' beside it, where he had lived; the Royal Baths / Marlborough House building; two cottages in Warwick Place; and four houses in Market Street, two in Ann Street and one in Egremont Place.[4]

But Trotter's overwhelming passion was the stage, and he regularly took the leading roles in the plays he produced at the Theatre Royal. In the 1813 edition of *A Sketch of Worthing* John Mackoull writes of the theatre and its proprietor as follows:

> There are few Country Theatres surpassing this either for construction or neatness. It was purchased by Mr Trotter, the present proprietor and manager, who is himself a respectable performer, but rather too gaunt a figure; he however makes up with the rest of his company what may be termed a good set of performers: and he generally gratifies the visitors and inhabitants during the season, by a succession of principal actors from the London and Bath theatres. The scenery and apparatus are excellent without being gaudy.

Mackoull, adds, however, that the 'gaming system' has had such an adverse effect on attendances at the theatre that sometimes the company 'has played, literally speaking, to empty benches' – and he suggests that 'there should be some regulation entered into' so that gambling is not permitted in Worthing on evenings when there are performances at the theatre.

Four years later Mackoull has for some reason fallen out of love with the theatre. The entire text of the section on the Theatre Royal in the 1817 edition of *A Sketch of Worthing* reads: 'As a provincial one we may say it is passable – and there it must rest for us. *Honi soit qui mal y pense.*'

As Mackoull's 1813 account suggests, many distinguished actors of the time did indeed appear at the Worthing theatre. One of these was Junius Brutus Booth, who was part of Trotter's company in 1815 and 1816, and whose roles included the title role in *Richard III* and Orlando

The Worthing Theatre

This anonymous sketch, dated 23 August 1818, is the best surviving early view of Worthing's first theatre, which opened in 1807. To the right is the garden in front of the single-storey cottage *orné* where Thomas Trotter, the theatre's first manager, lived. Both buildings were demolished in 1970, along with the rest of the north side of Ann Street.

The Theatre and Warwick House, *c.* 1810

This view by Jacob Spornberg looks east along Ann Street towards Warwick House. On the left is the theatre, and at centre-right is the northern end of the Colonnade.

Map of Worthing in 1814

This map, a crisper version of the map printed in the 1814 edition of John Evans's *A Picture of Worthing*, was prepared by Charles Smail for his son Henfrey's 1943 book, *The Worthing Road and its Coaches*. Among the significant additions since the conjectural map of Worthing in 1805 (page 47) are the new road from the north end of South Street past the recently-built Chapel of Ease to Worthing House; Market Street; the buildings on Ann Street; the terrace on the north side of Warwick Street; and the Steyne Hotel and Steyne Row. Stafford's Library has moved from Marine Place to the western half of the new building just west of the Steyne Hotel.

in *As You Like It*. In 1821 Booth abandoned his wife and young son and emigrated to the United States with his mistress, where he became one of the most celebrated actors in America and fathered ten more children. One of these was John Wilkes Booth, who also found fame on the stage – but much greater fame when he assassinated President Abraham Lincoln in 1865.

A theatre was not the only important facility lacking in Worthing when Edward Ogle arrived in the town. There was also no modern hotel, a serious failing in a town with any ambition to be an important resort. Visitors to Worthing were accommodated either in lodging-houses or in old-fashioned inns such as the Nelson Inn, the Sea House Inn and the New Inn, all three of which were located in South Street, the latter two opposite each other at the sea-end of the street.

These premises offered only limited accommodation. On 18 August 1805 a newspaper reported that the previous evening 'the sands had been crowded with carriages of various descriptions' belonging to 'a great party of nobility' which had come over from Brighton. There were 153 people in the party, far too many to be fed or accommodated in Worthing, for the report tells us that '27 persons dined at the house of Mr Hogsflesh [the Sea House Inn], and 15 at the house of Mr Bacon [the New Inn]' – we shall hear more of Hogsflesh and Bacon in Chapter 8 – while a few others were accommodated at the Nelson Inn in South Street. Over a hundred of the noble visitors, however, had to return to Brighton. The report added that 'this inconveniency will be removed next season, by the building of an hotel on a scale suitable to the dignity of the visitors'.[5]

This hotel, which was built on the site of an old inn at the south-west corner of today's Steyne Gardens, was part of Edward Ogle's ambitious plans for the western side of the parcel of land that separated his house from the seafront. This land, which Ogle had acquired as part of the Warwick House estate, had previously been part of Worthing manor and was known as Singers.[6] It was probably Ogle who named it the Steyne, in emulation of the Steine in Brighton. ('Steyne' was originally the spelling used in Brighton too.[7] The word comes from Old English *stoene*, meaning a stony place.) The naming seems to have taken place about 1808, since documents relating to No. 13, The Steyne, dated 5 January 1808, refer to its site as 'on the west side of a certain place called or intended to be called The Steyne'. Ogle was not only instrumental in setting in motion this major building project; he also retained the ownership of three houses in the Steyne, and most of the Steyne Hotel, of which he held ten of the sixteen shares. The hotel opened on 1 July 1807 and work on the rest of Steyne Row – which had the Worthing Bank situated at the northern end – appears to have started in 1807 and been completed the following year.[8]

An important feature of Ogle's new hotel was a large room that doubled as the hotel's ball-room and the town's Assembly Room, which opened on 23 September 1808. Today the Steyne Hotel forms the southern section of the Chatsworth Hotel, and the old Assembly Room has been sub-divided; but the room originally stretched from the front of the building to the back. It was decorated with an allegorical painting by Manaturi, and there was a superb chandelier of gilt bronze. There was also an organ, about which John Mackoull writes disparagingly in the 1813 edition of *A Sketch of Worthing*: 'There is an Orchestra, and an Organ; the Organ, however, is good for nothing, and appears more to tell us there should be one than any thing else.'

Mackoull is also scathing in his criticism of the Master of Ceremonies at the Assembly Room, one Mr Chandless, to whom he devotes no fewer than five pages. Mackoull claims that while Chandless remains in the role 'the fashionables will not assemble', and that the young people of Worthing go to the Assembly Room for the specific purpose of making fun of him. He says that Chandless's friends should tell him to retire – although, bizarrely, he then goes on to pay tribute to the 'many handsome things' that Chandless and his friends have said and done to promote Mackoull's own interests.

By the time of the 1817 edition of *A Sketch of Worthing* the hapless Mr Chandless has indeed 'relinquished the situation' and the position has been vacant 'a considerable time'. The problem, according to Mackoull, is that, while the Master of Ceremonies needs to be 'a real Gentleman both in manners and conversation', many people might take the view that 'no real Gentleman would accept such a situation, considering it as a degradation'. Mackoull does not share this view, although he now makes clear the reason for his evident prejudice against Chandless:

> There is one thing we would recommend, never to turn informer, backbiter, or slanderer, for then they become men of NO CEREMONY, despised and treated with that contempt they deserve, and hence arises the degradation.

Mackoull is never hesitant in expressing his prejudices, although, as in the case of Chandless, he sometimes disguises them by a show of even-handedness. One guesses that it was either Edward Ogle's majority shareholding in the Steyne Hotel or Mackoull's dislike of the hotel's manager that causes Mackoull to dismiss the hotel in a single sentence in the 1813 edition of *A Sketch of Worthing*, saying that the hotel 'is upon a large and extensive scale, and like all other hotels on the same plan, has its accommodations and disagreeables'. It is characteristic of Mackoull to hint at – but not specify – shortcomings, as also in the case of Warwick House (see page 18), in the expectation that his readers will draw their own conclusions.

By contrast, Mackoull is unstinting in his praise of the Sea House Inn – which he calls the Sea House Hotel, a name that was occasionally (though not normally) used for this relatively modest establishment. Perhaps it had been upgraded following its recent acquisition by Mr Parsons.[9] He tells us that the beds at the Sea House are as comfortable as anyone could wish, the wines 'are of the first vintage'; 'the larder contains eatables that would gratify the most studious epicure'; and 'the charges are reasonable'. By 1817 Mr Parsons has moved to the Steyne Hotel, and as a result Mackoull has totally revised his opinion of it: 'In point of accommodations there is no superior to the Steyne Hotel, it having undergone a most finished alteration.' A whole paragraph is devoted to the excellence of the wines.

In addition to building Steyne Row and the Steyne Hotel on land he owned, Edward Ogle sold numerous plots of land for others to build on – particularly on the north side of Warwick Street and on Mole Soals, a piece of land on the north side of Ann Street. Ann Street had been no more than a farm-track when Ogle arrived in Worthing, but by 1805 was 'a street or road called or intended to be called Ann Street', named after Ogle's wife. Ogle then sold this land plot by plot during his first ten years in Worthing.[10]

A town with a growing population needed proper provision of stabling, and once again Ogle was involved. The town's first commercial stables were built on land he sold for the purpose for £500 in January 1805. Edward and James Ogle – James's name appears in some documents involving Ogle property in Worthing – sold another patch of land on Ann Street for £630 to provide stables for the new Steyne Hotel, which were in place by the end of 1809. Ogle also bought a recently erected stables just to the north of the Steyne Mews on 12 July 1810 for £1,650 and rented it to the proprietor of the Steyne Hotel as additional stabling.[11]

As well as being the town's biggest landowner and developer, Edward Ogle was also active in the town's administration. When he arrived in Worthing, it was, as we saw earlier, still part of the parish of Broadwater, from which it was separated in 1803 by Act of Parliament; and Ogle almost certainly played a leading part in bringing about this legislation. (The preamble to this act stated that the 'hamlet' of Worthing should in future be known as a town.) Certainly when the new Board of Commissioners for Worthing met for the first time on 13 June 1803, at the Nelson Inn in South Street, Edward Ogle – although he had been a resident of the town for only

Steyne Field and Steyne Row
This watercolour, which dates from soon after the Steyne Hotel (at sea-end) and Steyne Row were built in 1807–8, shows that the newly named Steyne Field initially remained a meadow. The prominent sign on the right of the picture, reading 'To the Steyne Hotel', suggests that the picture may have been painted for the Steyne Hotel's manager or for Edward Ogle, the majority shareholder.

Steyne Hotel
Although this engraving of the Steyne Hotel dates from 1849, it shows the hotel just as it was in its early days. Its original simple Georgian appearance changed in the 1860s when the south façade of the hotel was given bay windows. The Stafford's Library / Rebecca House building to its west received similar treatment at about the same time.

The Chapel of Ease in 1822
The Chapel of Ease – later St Paul's church – was built to spare the people of Worthing the mile and a quarter journey to Broadwater for Sunday worship. It opened in 1812, and was 'christened' in June 1813. In its early days it was separate from the main part of Worthing, which can be seen in the distance.

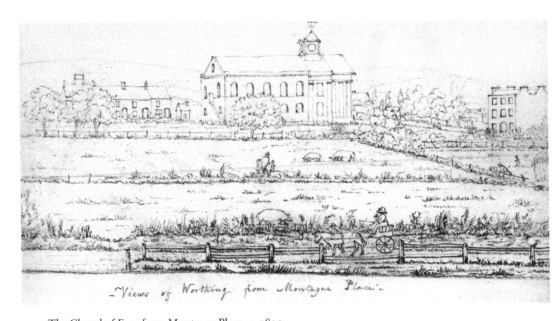

The Chapel of Ease from Montague Place, *c.* 1820
This view, looking north from Montague Place towards the Chapel of Ease, reminds us how much agricultural land there still was in the heart of Worthing. This remained the case until the 1860s.

two years – was the Chairman. At the second meeting, on 29 June, the important decision was taken to lay a brick drain along the length of Worthing as it then existed, with cesspools every hundred feet – a long-overdue provision.[12]

It was also 'at the instance of' Edward Ogle that the town acquired its market in 1810.[13] The Act authorising the market specified that none of the town commissioners should benefit financially from the project, but part of the land to be used was owned by Edward Ogle and part by his fellow-commissioner Richard Cook. Ogle and Cook sold their parcels of land to a man called James Hopkins for £514-10s and £294 respectively. The two commissioners had thus covered their position while indirectly making money from the project. Hopkins then sold the combined land to the commissioners for £1,050, so making a handsome profit – although, oddly, the final land deal was not completed until some six weeks after the newly built market opened on 2 July 1810.[14]

John Mackoull, writing in 1813, is full of praise for what he refers to as 'the market-house', the main entrance to which was on the north side of Ann Street, just to the east of the front garden of Thomas Trotter's cottage *orné*. He describes it as 'a handsome, clean, well-built place, exceeding well regulated'. Eggs, butter, fruit and vegetables are 'always in abundance, and of the first quality', and 'every encouragement is given to keep up the regular supplies of fish, flesh, and fowl'. However although the fish-sellers try to ensure that the price of fish is reasonable, 'this it is much lamented they cannot always accomplish; and it frequently happens *from some unknown cause, that fish is enormously dear*'. This unknown cause may have been the idle and dissolute ways of the town's fishermen, of whom Mackoull has this to say in a later section of his book:

> The boatmen or fishermen of Worthing chiefly employ themselves in the mackerel and herring season; after which they return to a life of indolence, and seem to be extremely blest, if they have been able to procure enough for the maintenance of their families during the winter. They have little or no idea of saving against what is termed a rainy day, but generally expend their hard earned gains in temporary dissipation.

A piece of land of which Ogle was careful to retain ownership was Steyne Field – now Steyne Gardens – which provided an open aspect between Warwick House and the sea. Ogle held this land on a copyhold rather than a freehold basis. By the early nineteenth century the main difference between freehold and copyhold was that copyholders had to pay a notional rent to the Manor and a 'fine' when they sold the property. Ogle's copyhold ownership of Steyne Field included a restrictive covenant by which the owner undertook to maintain the land as pleasure gardens.[15] It was on this field that, as described on page 29, a skirmish occurred in September 1812 after Ogle and his friends tried to stop the band of the South Bramber Volunteers playing there.

The following year Edward Ogle proved more generous in a matter of a musical nature. Although no longer part of Broadwater parish for administrative purposes from 1803, Worthing did not have a separate church until the Chapel of Ease – later St Paul's church – was built in 1812. The original organ was donated by Ogle. The pseudonymous local poet Paul Potion makes a complimentary reference to the instrument, in lines characterised by his usual arbitrary use of italics and, in this case, capitals as well:

> Or if *above* you go to pray'rs,
> You must ascend the *gall'ry* stairs;
> In which you may, where'er you be,
> A small, neat, fine ton'd ORGAN see;

'SQUIRE OGLE'S gift, as we are told
By an inscription – *black and gold!*

After 1812 there is little information about Ogle's activities in Worthing. Perhaps he felt that his job in the town was largely done, and again devoted more time to his and his brother's interests in London. Perhaps he was content to let the energetic Thomas Trotter take over where he had left off – and in any case the second decade of the century was largely a period of consolidation for Worthing.

From the Wellington Inn to York Terrace
Although this engraving probably dates from 1830–35, this section of the seafront is almost exactly as it was during the second decade of the nineteenth century. The building on the left is the Wellington Inn, which until *c.* 1816 had been a house called Marine Cottage. The low building to its right probably dates from a few years before the engraving was done. The other buildings are, left to right: Great Terrace, Little Terrace, the Stafford's Library / Rebecca House building, the Steyne Hotel, and York Terrace (*c.* 1823).

Chapter 7

The Life and Grievances of John Mackoull

Like many men of purpose and initiative – and perhaps a dash of arrogance – Edward Ogle was not universally popular, and the episode involving the band of the South Bramber Volunteers described in Chapter 2 suggests that he could be autocratic. As we have seen, it was John Mackoull, obsessive in his hatred of the town's chief citizen, who was responsible for most of the adverse comment about Ogle that has come down to us, although there were doubtless others in Worthing who to some extent shared his views.

Mackoull is such an extraordinary character that no history of early Worthing would be complete without a full account of him.

John Mackoull was 'a plain rogue' who belonged to a well-known criminal family from London. His mother was a shop-lifter and thief known as 'Gunpowder'.[1] The family name seems correctly to have been McCoull, the variant spelling possibly having been adopted by John in order to distance himself from his past. However 'Mackoull' was also used for other members of his family in some contemporary documents, so for the sake of simplicity we will use it throughout.

Although Gunpowder Mackoull's husband was a respectable tradesman, all her children – three sons and two daughters – became criminals. One son, Ben, was hanged for robbery in 1786. Another, James, a pickpocket, receiver of stolen goods and bank-robber, had a long criminal career in both Britain and Europe. He learnt German, and is said to have often played billiards with the Grand Duke of Mecklenburg-Schwerin and relieved him of large sums of money. He was a man of extraordinary affrontery, who sued in court for the return of money he had stolen when he and two accomplices had robbed the Paisley Union Bank of Glasgow in 1811. This was his undoing, however, for evidence was then found to prove that he had committed the crime and he was sentenced to death in 1820 and, although reprieved, died in prison.

James Mackoull was also suspected of the murder in Edinburgh in November 1806 of a man called Begbie, a porter with the British Linen Company Bank. Begbie was on the way to the head office of his bank with £4,000 in cash when he was killed. He was found with a knife plunged into his chest – the knife had been wrapped in soft paper to prevent blood getting onto the killer – and the money, needless to say, was missing. Many years later, in 1820, a Bow Street Runner named Denovan concluded from a description he had been given that the murderer was James Mackoull. Discovering that Mackoull was in prison in Edinburgh for the Paisley Union Bank robbery, Denovan went to interview him there and put it to him that he had been living near the scene of the crime in 1806. At this, James Mackoull 'seemed to rave and lose all temper'.[2]

John Mackoull's talents were more diverse than those of his brothers. He was certainly himself involved in criminal activity, but he was also a well-read man, whose writings, although often intemperate in tone, show a vigorous command of language. Indeed the intelligent and charismatic Mackoull comes across as the kind of semi-gentleman criminal who might have featured in the pages of Charles Dickens.

Which, as it happens, he did.

After the death in 1837 of Joseph Grimaldi – the 'Clown of Clowns, the greatest of them all ... [a man of] incomparable genius'[3] – Grimaldi's memoirs came into the hands of Richard Bentley, the editor of *Bentley's Miscellany*, in which Dickens's second novel, *Oliver Twist*, was then being serialised. Bentley asked the twenty-five-year-old author to turn the manuscript into something publishable.[4] Dickens was reluctant to take on the project because he thought it was 'very badly done' and 'redolent of twaddle', and agreed only on condition that he was paid the substantial sum of £300.

The book was published in 1838 as 'Edited by Boz', with illustrations by Dickens's usual illustrator, George Cruikshank. In his introduction, Dickens sets out his approach to the task, saying that he has edited the book 'to the best of his ability, altering its form throughout, and making such other alterations as ... would improve the narration of the facts, without any departure from the facts themselves'. It is fairly clear that Dickens added some novelistic colour to the account, and much of the dialogue has a Dickensian ring to it.

More than forty pages[5] of *Memoirs of Joseph Grimaldi* are taken up with Grimaldi's acquaintance with John Mackoull, whom he knew as Mackintosh. The story is in effect told twice, first through Grimaldi's eyes and then – in a nine-page appendix to Chapter XIII – through Mackoull's. In the part of the narrative based on Grimaldi's manuscript, Mackoull is always referred to as Mackintosh, and Grimaldi seemingly never knew that this was an alias. It is only in the appendix that Dickens reveals that Mackintosh was really Mackoull. The source for the material Dickens used in the appendix was a book written by Mackoull, first published in 1809, whose full title – at least in the 'corrected and enlarged' second edition of 1812, which runs to 239 pages – was *Abuses of Justice / Illustrated by My Own Case / Disclosing Various Practices of the Officers of Criminal Law / With an Account of Several Interesting Trials / Anecdotes of Certain Bankers / And Hairbreadth Escapes of the Innocent and Guilty / Being a Vindication of the Author / From Several Charges of Forgery.*

Mackoull's account is of labyrinthine complexity, and following it is not made easier by the fact that almost all the – numerous – criminals that appear in its pages had aliases. The summary that follows of Mackoull's association with Grimaldi therefore takes its information from the two separate narratives (in the main text and in the appendix to Chapter XIII) in *Memoirs of Joseph Grimaldi*. In order to avoid confusion, the name 'Mackoull' is used throughout.

It was in November 1804 that Joseph Grimaldi first met John Mackoull. Mackoull had invited Jack Bologna, an actor friend of Grimaldi's, to come down to Kent for some shooting, and to bring a companion with him. Bologna had been led to believe that Mackoull was a 'large landed proprietor and that he had most splendid preserves'. Grimaldi was thus surprised, on their arrival in Bromley, to encounter 'a man in a fustian jacket, driving a tax-cart drawn by a very lame little horse' and to be greeted over-familiarly with a loud 'Hallo!' followed by 'Well, Joe, here you are!'

Grimaldi was further astonished to discover that the place where they were staying was a road-side public house, with a sign displaying the words 'Good Entertainment for Man and Beast'. Even this modest establishment – it was the George in Hayes, still a public house today – turned out to be owned not by Mackoull, but by his mother. However Grimaldi was on the whole amused rather than annoyed by all this, and indeed found 'something hearty and pleasant in the man's manner, despite his coarseness'.

The next day Grimaldi and Bologna were taken to the game preserves that Mackoull had promised them, expecting to see pheasants and partridges, but were shown into a field full of pigeons. The two men made the best of the situation, and shot a large number of the birds. As soon as they had picked up the dead pigeons, however, Mackoull suggested that they 'cut away

Above: The George Inn, Hayes, in 1818
This was the inn near Bromley in Kent where the actors Joseph Grimaldi and Jack Bologna stayed in November 1804 at the invitation of John Mackoull, whom they knew as Mackintosh. The pub was owned and run by his mother, 'Gunpowder' Mackoull. The village stocks are visible at the right of the picture.

Right: Mr Mackintosh's Covey
In this illustration by George Cruikshank (1792–1898) from Charles Dickens's 1838 biography of Joseph Grimaldi, John Mackoull – alias Mackintosh – is showing Bologna and Grimaldi the shooting he has brought them down from London to enjoy, which turns out to involve pigeons rather than the pheasants and partridges they had expected.

Joseph Grimaldi (1778–1837)
This portrait of Joseph Grimaldi by John Cawse (*c.* 1779-1862) dates from 1807, the same year that Grimaldi attended John Mackoull's trial at Stafford assizes. (© National Portrait Gallery, London)

at once' as otherwise the squire would have them put in prison – upon which it became clear that they had been shooting on land over which Mackoull had no rights.

Back in London the following day, Grimaldi and Bologna went to the Garrick's Head in Bow Street and were laughing about their adventures when the gamekeeper from Hayes, a man called Clarke, entered the inn. Clarke had discovered that the 'rascals' who had killed his employer's pigeons had been staying at the George, and had spoken to Mackoull; and Mackoull had told him that the culprits were actors from London – 'one's a clown and t' other's a harlequin'. So Clarke had come up to London to find them. The situation was potentially serious, but the landlord of the Garrick's Head, a friend of Clarke's, handled it so adroitly that the man was pacified by a good meal of steak and wine and an offer to pay for the pigeons; and Grimaldi and Bologna were even invited back to Kent for a proper day's shooting.

Grimaldi heard no more of Mackoull for over two years until, in January 1807, Mackoull unexpectedly called on him in London and apologised for 'the little trick he had played in mere thoughtlessness' two years before. He told Grimaldi that his mother had sold the public house, and that he himself had now become involved in business and was living in Throgmorton Street in the City. Mackoull had changed considerably since Grimaldi had seen him last: 'His appearance was extremely smart, his manners were greatly improved, and altogether he had acquired much polish and refinement.' Grimaldi invited him to dinner with him and his wife Mary, and Mackoull's conversation proved so 'jocose and amusing' that he was asked back on several occasions.

In due course Mackoull took Grimaldi to dine with some friends of his at a very large house in Charlotte Street, 'where everything was on a scale of the most costly splendour'. Luxurious food and expensive wines were served by 'numerous attendants in handsome liveries'. The others present were six ladies and six gentlemen. All the ladies wore 'jewellery of the most brilliant description', and Grimaldi was much impressed by 'the politeness of the gentlemen and the graceful ease of the ladies'. There were several further such dinners, and the Grimaldis invited their impressive new friends back to their own house, in spite of Mary Grimaldi's embarrassment at having 'not one quarter so many spoons as the Charlotte Street people, and no chandeliers at all'.

Then, on the night of 12–13 March, £4,500 in bank-notes and bills of credit were stolen from the Edinburgh mail-coach. Some of the bills were passed on to a man called Knight, who exchanged them at various banks in the Midlands and the North, including at a bank in Congleton on 19 March. Mackoull, who bore a close resemblance to Knight, was arrested on 3 April and charged with robbing the mail-coach and forging the endorsements on the bills. Luckily, however, Mackoull had been in Woolwich on the evening of 13 March, watching Grimaldi in *Don Juan*, so could not have robbed the mail-coach twenty-four hours earlier; and on the evening of 18 March Grimaldi had been with him till eleven o'clock, so Mackoull could not have been the man who had exchanged the bills of credit in Congleton the following day.

Grimaldi and his wife agreed to provide alibi evidence – which was supported by others – but the prosecution, egged on by a man called Kensington, the proprietor of the bank that had lost the money, persisted with the case. After a number of hearings at Bow Street Magistrates' Court, the case was set for trial at Stafford assizes and Mackoull, finally given bail, called on Grimaldi to thank him for his help. Grimaldi suggested that it might have a favourable effect on the jury if Mackoull's rich friends could be present in court. To this Mackoull replied that they would not come if sent for, and that if they did it would harm his case – and he then told Grimaldi the truth about the six Charlotte Street couples.

None of the women were married to the men, and all the men were criminals. Farmer, the host at the dinners, had been 'sentenced to death at the Old Bailey, and got a reprieve while standing on the drop below the gallows'. Williams was a forger. Jesson and Barber were burglars. 'And the

Jewish-looking man who sings Kelly's songs?'[6] asked Grimaldi. 'Oh, he helps to pass the forged notes and has been three times in the pillory.' The final man, Jones, was the man who had robbed the stage-coach.[7] (Dickens does not explore the implications of the fact that the stage-coach robber was a close associate of Mackoull's.)

Although Grimaldi was furious that he and his wife had been deceived into spending time with 'such a horde of villains', he was too good and honourable a man not to do the right thing by an innocent man who stood in peril of the gallows, since four of the five crimes with which Mackoull was charged were capital offences.

In order to attend the trial at Stafford, which was held in August 1807, Grimaldi had to take several days off from his duties at Sadler's Wells theatre, where he was playing the clown in a pantomime called *Jan Ben Jan, or Harlequin and the Forty Virgins*. A man referred to as 'Bradbury of the Circus' took his place.

No fewer than nine prosecution witnesses were present in court, and all of them identified Mackoull as the offender. It seems unlikely that nine honest witnesses could all have been mistaken, so they were probably other criminals with a grudge against Mackoull or were being paid by the banker Kensington. Grimaldi was subjected to fierce cross-examination, but, according to Mackoull, 'those who expected to see the zany[8] disgrace himself by his buffoonery beheld him deliver his evidence with a firmness which could only arise from conscious rectitude'. The prosecuting counsel tried to discredit Mackoull and the Grimaldis – Mary Grimaldi also gave evidence – by alleging that Mackoull kept 'disorderly houses' (that is, brothels) and suggesting that the Grimaldis were involved in a 'foul conspiracy to defeat justice'. Fortunately Mr Justice Graham found the Grimaldis' evidence persuasive, and in his summing-up told the jury that it was his view that the prosecution witnesses had mistaken Mackoull for the real culprit. The jury concurred and, at the end of a nine-hour trial, Mackoull was found not guilty.

After the trial Grimaldi – who emerges with much credit from this episode – spoke to Mackoull for a few minutes, urging him to reform his ways as, although innocent on this occasion, he would otherwise inevitably end up in serious trouble. Grimaldi told Mackoull that, while they could not again meet socially, Mackoull should write to him if he ever needed help. However Grimaldi never heard from Mackoull again – and indeed before long Mackoull had left behind the criminal temptations of London to settle on the Sussex coast.

...

Soon after arriving in Worthing Mackoull set himself up in an establishment he called the Apollo Music and Classical Library. This was originally on the edge of the town, in Chapel Street (today the southern section of Portland Road), but by 1813 Mackoull had relocated to South Street. In addition to running his library, he wrote and published three editions (1811, 1813 and 1817) of *A Sketch of Worthing*, his idiosyncratic guide to the town, each of them markedly different from the others, and with different full titles. The author's name does not appear, but the books have the publisher credit 'J. Mackoull, Apollo Library'.

In the 1817 edition of *A Sketch of Worthing* Mackoull refers to his having been slandered by the town's citizens 'for near eight years'. This phrase indicates that he was certainly in Worthing by about 1809; but, since there was initially a benign period for him after his arrival – and we do not know how long that was – he may in fact have arrived quite soon after his acquittal in Stafford. Either way, his past in due course began to cause difficulties for him, as he explains:

> Acting under the advice of my friends, I quitted London and commenced business as a Stationer,
> Librarian, and Music-Seller, at Worthing, where I soon gained the good-will and attention of

my neighbours. After some time, however, I experienced an unaccountable reserve and coldness in their behaviour, and many withdrew from their former habits of intercourse and sociability, without any apparent reason. … Anonymous letters, many of which containing the most abominable falsehoods, to stigmatize and lessen me in the estimation of my neighbours, had been industriously dispersed through Worthing and its vicinity. … Wherever I went, persecution pursued me, and I continually found myself the butt at which its malevolent shafts were levelled.[9]

Worse was to follow. Mackoull says that several members of what he refers to as 'the Dudfield gang' then visited Worthing and 'endeavoured by dint of unfounded assertion to traduce and injure me'. (According to Mackoull the criminals involved in the stage-coach robbery and its aftermath were Treble, the actual robber; Dudfield, who had 'received the bills of exchange'; and Knight, who had 'negotiated' them at various banks.) Kensington the banker also came down to Worthing to make trouble. The Dudfield gang apparently had a devious plan to exact revenge for Mackoull's having exposed them in the original 1809 edition of *Abuses of Justice*. Treble travelled to Sussex to pass off stolen bills of exchange – two in Worthing and one in Arundel – in the hope that Mackoull would be implicated. However, at a further bank where he tried to exchange a bill, suspicions were aroused and Treble was questioned and his hotel room searched. It became clear that he had altered his appearance by wearing a wig of a different colour from his own hair. He was arrested, and found to be in possession of various stolen and forged bills, as well as numerous other wigs. He was sentenced to death, but hanged himself in prison before the sentence could be carried out.[10]

In view of the fact that Mackoull brought so much criminal baggage to the quiet and respectable sea-side resort of Worthing, it is not surprising that he did not find favour with the upright and somewhat autocratic Edward Ogle; and the ten years or so that Mackoull spent in Worthing were overshadowed by a feud between the two men.

Mackoull's account of the skirmish between Edward Ogle and the band of the South Bramber Volunteers (see pages 27–29) is, of course, not impartial, and we learn more about Mackoull's dislike of Ogle from the 1817 edition of his guide to Worthing. The full title of this edition was *A Sketch of Worthing / As It Was and Now Is / and the Places Adjacent / Containing Useful and Necessary Observations on Men and Things / with a Topographical Description of the Places of Note on the Journey from London to Worthing / Intended as a Vade Mecum for Those who Visit this Delightful Place*.

The book opens with an extraordinary preface, entitled 'To the Public', in which Mackoull inveighs against certain people in the town (although no-one is named, it is certainly Ogle and Ogle's allies that he has in his sights):

The author having been attacked by a set of characters denominated *Gentlemen Touters* from the *first moment* he made his appearance at Worthing (as a Librarian and Stationer) to the present moment, by their *pulling, hauling, tearing, lying,* and *slandering* him for near eight years, has ruined him in his finances – a circumstance he understands gives the *Gentlemen Touters a pleasing satisfaction*. How far this pleasantry and rejoicing may last – is a question, and will be better seen and answered when a publication under 'the Title of a Sharp look out; or Characters in Worthing' makes its appearance.

(Sadly the further book Mackoull promised seems never to have been published – perhaps even he gave some thought to the possible consequences of defamatory excess.)

Mackoull's preface is only the beginning. He then embarks on a bizarre tour of Worthing and the surrounding area, with digressions far longer than the brief passages of useful information about the town itself. In the section entitled 'The Bank', Worthing's bank merits just one paragraph, before Mackoull launches into a four-page diatribe about the way he was treated by Kensington and Co of Lombard Street in 1807, which ends: 'And here we rest our grievances, silently mourning our disastrous fate, that should have placed us against such fiends in human shape.' In the section on 'Lawyers' – and, remember, this is meant to be a guide to Worthing – Mackoull notes in a single sentence that there are four lawyers in the town, and then devotes eight pages to inveighing against the profession in general and going back over the events of 1807, lamenting that the two lawyers that Kensington hired were, respectively, 'a horrible character' and 'a celebrated Sharp Practitioner'.

Finally, Mackoull returns, in the last twelve pages of his 108-page book, to the question of 'touting', in two chapters entitled 'Touting or Touters' and 'Gentlemen Touters'. The former appear to be local tradesmen who cheat visitors; the second are those citizens of Worthing who slander and harass him. Mackoull claims that they have ruined him and 'prevented [him] from educating and supporting three children no better than orphans and supporting an aged mother upwards of 90 years old'. (It would appear that 'Gunpowder' Mackoull was spending her retirement in Worthing.)

Mackoull was clearly much embittered by the fact that he was still, as he saw it, being persecuted after he had followed Grimaldi's kindly advice and made a determined effort to live a life of virtue. Both he and Ogle were driven and obsessive men, but very different in character. It was a clash of Cavalier and Roundhead. Although Mackoull's books are full of bitterness and anger, much of the warm-heartedness that charmed Grimaldi remains. He clearly loved Worthing, and he is generous in his praise of many of his fellow-townsmen, including the town's inn-keepers and hoteliers; the three doctors, particularly Dr Morrah; and the proprietors of the town's 'assinary', who looked after their donkeys unusually well – Mackoull observing that cruelty to animals 'betrays a littleness of mind, and a depraved heart'.

Although Mackoull does not use Ogle's name in his chapters about touters, he specifies his enemy in the section on Warwick House, which says little about the house but concentrates on

Three Worthing Scenes

These three prints date from about 1825. In the view on the facing page, part of York Terrace, erected *c.* 1823 is visible at far right, followed (right to left) by the Steyne Hotel, the Rebecca House / Stafford's Library building, Little Terrace, and Great Terrace. The second picture shows Wicks's Warm Baths, with Montpelier Terrace to its left. The third picture is a view of South Street, in which the three principal inns in Worthing in the early nineteenth century can be seen: the protruding sign on the left marks the Nelson Inn, while the New Inn and the Sea House Inn are at the end of the street, on the left and the right respectively. The second and third pictures are versions, with different figures, of the prints reproduced on page 37 and the front cover of this book. There is no way of knowing which versions were the earlier.

making – to use the phrase from his book's title – 'useful and necessary observations' on the character and activities of Edward Ogle (the original punctuation is preserved):

> Warwick House, situated at the bottom of High Street, commands a very interesting view, but in point of accommodations, 'it is not what it seemd' – It was built by a gentleman named Luther, and sold by him to Lord Warwick, who disposed of it to J. W. Commerell, from whom it afterwards came to the present possessor, a Mr. Ogle.
> 'There is a tide in the affairs of men,
> 'Which, taken at the flood, leads on to fortune.
> It is better to be born fortunate, than rich, some men are plodding and toiling all their lives, and can scarce make a living – another, whose mind is blunted, and who scarcely possesses two ideas, shall jump from beggary into affluence by one fortunate stroke. – It is not then, the shrewd or industrious man, that always succeeds in life – it is the fortunate. – Warwick House and its appurtenances was a bargain indeed! – The present owner from the magnitude of the purchase, obtained the sovereignity of Worthing, and is ycleped [called] King Ogle – to be great is to be good, to be good is to be great.

In view of what we know of his past, the author's attempt to identify himself with luckless plodders and toilers who can hardly make a living carries little conviction; and it is still more absurd to refer to the brilliant and enterprising Edward Ogle as a man 'whose mind is blunted, and who scarcely possesses two ideas'.

Mackoull continues: 'His Majesty ranks high in literary attainments, a work entitled the Picture of Worthing, with plates, has been presented to the public, at the moderate price of ten shillings and sixpence!' He claims that 'nearly the whole edition has been deposited in the archives of Warwick House', sarcastically suggesting that a possible explanation for the book's failure to sell is that 'the public is wanting in discernment, and cannot discover the merits of the production'. He adds that 'the indignant author' is said to have 'commented in bitter terms' that he had 'thrown pearl before swine' – whereupon Mackoull mock-consoles him with the reflection that the works of great writers such as Milton and Butler,[11] 'whose works are now idolised', were initially also undervalued. He notes that one 'ill-natured critic [probably Mackoull himself] recommended the work to be sold by weight'.

Mackoull's venom against this book was no doubt mainly due to its being a rival to his own guide-book. An oddity, however, is the fact that the book in question is clearly John Evans's *A Picture of Worthing*, whose second edition had appeared in 1814. It is possible that the paranoid Mackoull thought that it had been written by Ogle under a pseudonym, but, as we saw in Chapter 1, this was certainly not the case, since Evans was entirely genuine – although it may be that Ogle had in effect commissioned the book.

Another reason for Mackoull's vendetta against Ogle was doubtless that Ogle was a rival and probably more successful library-owner. Unsurprisingly, he uses *A Sketch of Worthing* to promote his own establishment, and in the section on libraries in the 1813 edition he gives a detailed – if oddly punctuated – list of what is available at the Apollo Library, including 'musical instruments of the first description, viz. Piano Fortes, Harps, Violins, Flutes, Flageolets, (single or double,) for sale or on hire'. Sheet music as well as books may be borrowed, and Mackoull gives the charges, and then goes on to advertise what else is available:

> Stationery and fancy ornaments of every description. Perfumery of the best quality. Likewise may be had at the Apollo Library, Night and Day Telescopes, on the latest improvements, port-folios of Caricatures, Magic Lanthorns, Chess, Drafts, and Back-gammon boards, &c. for the

evening. Gentlemen provided with fishing tackle, fowling pieces, and every other necessary apparatus for shooting.

Mackoull then dismisses Worthing's other two libraries in a single sentence: 'The other libraries are Mrs. Spooner's, at the Colonade [*sic*], and Mr Stafford's, near the Steyne: at these toys may be purchased.'

In a more general section that follows, entitled 'Circulating Libraries', Mackoull briefly discusses the history of libraries, of which he says there are now at least a thousand in Britain. He then returns to his competitors in Worthing, criticising them for having recently introduced 'gaming', which he describes as 'one of the most destructive vices of society' and results in 'music, books, and conversation' being 'banished from these places'. The gaming in question consists of visitors to the library paying a shilling or half-a-crown 'to raffle for an article, which should *you win*, is very short of the value laid on it'. Mackoull claims that 'it is a well known fact that last season one gentleman and his friends were so very fortunate as to take away nearly all the principal articles'. He is probably suggesting that Edward Ogle fixed the raffles at the Colonnade Library so that he and his friends won the prizes. (These raffles in fact cannot have been as recently introduced as Mackoull suggests, since, as we saw in Chapter 3, Jane Austen won seventeen shillings at a raffle held at either Spooner's or Stafford's Library on 19 September 1805.)

But the inter-library rivalries in Regency Worthing seem not to have stopped with each establishment competing to offer the most tempting diversions, for in the 1817 edition of *A Sketch of Worthing* Mackoull implies that his own library has suffered as the result of unscrupulous behaviour on the part of the other two library proprietors:

> We have occasion to observe, that these places frequently become a scene of slanderous warfare, and of ill natured observations, from a disposition of gaining a preference – for a series of years it has been kept up in a most infamous and shameful manner, we therefore caution our readers against this sort of conduct, that when the poisonous tongue of malignancy dares to assail their ears, either by the production of infamous anonymous hand-bills or artful insinuations, they will have recourse to their own senses, and not suffer themselves as it is termed by the calumniators to be *Earwiged*.

(The italicised – and mis-spelt – word 'Earwiged' sounds like a deliberate half-echo of Edward Ogle's name.)

From all that we know of Ogle he was a pillar of rectitude. He obviously regarded Mackoull as an undesirable presence in Worthing, and possibly he did everything he could to drive him out. Nonetheless Ogle does not come across as the kind of man who would have been responsible for 'anonymous hand-bills'. We know nothing of Stafford, the owner of the library on the seafront, and perhaps he was a less scrupulous individual; but there were probably a number of people in the town who were ill-disposed towards Mackoull and could have been responsible for the hand-bills.

Mackoull's grievance against the 'gentlemen touters' owes to the fact that they had persecuted him on the basis of his enemies' version of past events. But there was clearly no shortage of material for 'artful insinuations' against Mackoull, and these may have included the suggestion that the Apollo Music and Classical Library had at one point offered, in addition to the usual music and gambling, the kind of entertainment that had been available in the disorderly houses Mackoull had kept in London. Certainly there is a curious passage in the 1817 edition of *A Sketch of Worthing* where Mackoull notes, seemingly with regret, that 'Characters denominated

Impures seldom make their appearance here', the local clergyman having '*sought out* and routed these intruders' and 'declared that no *naughty women* shall have a resting place in Worthing'.

The feud between Mackoull and Ogle, which must have divided opinion in Worthing, and indeed been the cause of much gossip, ended with Ogle's death in March 1819. By a curious coincidence, John Mackoull went bankrupt at almost exactly the same time. In the *New Monthly Magazine* of 1 March 1819 The entry 'J. Mackoull, Worthing, Sussex, stationer, Feb. 9' appears in the list of names in the section entitled 'Dividends' (this being the term used for the distribution of funds to creditors at the end of the bankruptcy process).

The historical record affords us one final glimpse of John Mackoull.

A passage in the Newgate Calendar of 1828 makes clear that Mackoull had not genuinely become a reformed character after he published *Abuses of Justice* in 1809: 'His contrition, however, may be doubted; for in 1820, he was the proprietor of two brothels in London and of the Apollo circulating library in Worthing, Sussex.'[12]

Although the date 1820 is incorrect for the Worthing enterprise – as we have seen, Mackoull was declared bankrupt the previous year – it would appear from this reference that at some point he returned to brothel-keeping. Perhaps, like Edward Ogle, he had business interests both in London and in Worthing during the 1810s. Or perhaps it was after the Apollo Library closed that, despairing of respectable endeavour, he returned to London and went back to employing 'characters denominated impures'.

Since his mother was over ninety in 1817, Mackoull himself was probably in his sixties by this time, so perhaps he did not long survive his great enemy, Ogle; but the date of his death is not recorded. It is ironic that someone so noisy and so theatrical, and of whose life and opinions we know so much – both from his own effusions and from the account in the pages of Dickens's biography of Grimaldi – should have left the stage so unobtrusively.

Chapter 8
Seven Notable Visitors

Robert Bloomfield

The poet Robert Bloomfield is of interest to us not only because he visited Worthing in the summer of 1805 – indeed he may have been in the town at the same time as Jane Austen – but also because his view of the English seaside has been compared to hers by the literary critic B. C. Southam:

> In general Jane Austen's observation of seaside manners has a note of gaiety, not unlike the tone of Bloomfield's 'News from Worthing', a gently satirical account of the poet's delight at the flirtatiousness of the visiting young ladies. In *Sanditon*, however, the satire is also directed far more acutely at what Jane Austen sensed as an uneasy spirit of change. Her story is full of migrant figures, of visitors in search of health, profit, or fashionable company.[1]

Bloomfield, who came from a humble background in Suffolk, left school at the age of eleven to work on a local farm and later as a shoemaker, and it was there that he developed his interest in poetry. His most famous poem, 'The Farmer's Boy', published in 1800, sold 26,000 copies in three years, but is remembered today mainly for the fact that John Constable used couplets from it as 'tags' for two of his paintings; and for two famous lines:

> Strange to the world, he bore a bashful look,
> The Fields his study, Nature was his book.

Robert Bloomfield seems to have been a rather sad and muddled individual. Even the famously warm-hearted Charles Lamb – whose own association with Worthing will be described in a moment – wrote to a friend that Bloomfield was 'a damn'd stupid hound in company'. After Bloomfield's death, however, Lamb wrote more kindly of him, saying: 'He dined with me once, and his manners took me exceedingly.'

When Bloomfield submitted 'News from Worthing' to the editor of *The Monthly Mirror*, the journal in which it was published in April 1807, he sent the following accompanying letter:

> Sir,
> The lines I now send you were written in an idle hour, at Worthing, in the summer of 1805. Several MS copies are abroad, and they may possibly find their way into print. I, therefore, deeming it essential to have even nonsense printed correctly, offer them for your acceptance.
> And am yours, &c.
> Robert Bloomfield.

Bloomfield's son Charles had an intractable and painful knee infection that was of much concern to the family, and his wife had taken the boy to Worthing at the end of 1804 in the hope that the sea air would be beneficial.[2] Bloomfield's own visit at some point in the summer of 1805 may therefore also have related to his son's medical needs. The light-hearted poem he wrote during his stay takes the form of a verse letter supposedly composed by a female donkey to her brother. Below the poem Bloomfield adds an appreciative note about the kindly Mrs Spooner, who ran the Colonnade Library.

The poem is worth printing in full, since it offers a charming and evocative picture of both the place and the time:

NEWS FROM WORTHING,
IN A LETTER FROM A BEAST OF BURDEN TO HER BROTHER JACK

Brother Jack, I am going to inform you
Of things that ne'er enter'd your head,
And I hope the narration will charm you
Wherever you're driven or led;

For it grieves me to think of your hampers,
And the cudgel that thumps you behind;
You have none of my frolics and scampers,
My labour's as light as the wind.

On a fine level, form'd by the tide,
The beach and the ocean between,
Fashion here tells young lasses to ride
On the best walk that ever was seen.

The sands, brother Jack, that's the spot
Where the ladies exhibit their graces;
There they push me along till I trot,
Midst a circle of giggling faces.

Not one of the party stands idle,
For, when I move just like a snail,
One half of them pull at my bridle,
And t' other half push at my tail.

Then up, full of frolic and glee,
One will mount, and will scold, and will strike,
And ride me knee deep in the sea,
Where I stop – just as long as I like.

For what are their tricks and manoeuvres?
They may pull me, and haul me, and tease,
But I plague them as they plague their lovers,
O, I like to do just as I please!

Travelling to Worthing by Coach
Most visitors to Worthing in the first quarter of the nineteenth century who did not have their own transport would have travelled to the town in – or on – a coach such as this.

News from Worthing
This supposed view of Worthing, which was printed in *The Monthly Mirror* in April 1807 to accompany Robert Bloomfield's poem 'News from Worthing', was clearly drawn by someone who had never visited the town, since there was no steep down beside Worthing beach, nor a church close to the sea.

Robert Bloomfield (1766–1823)
Robert Bloomfield wrote his
light-hearted poem 'News from
Worthing' after a visit to the
town in the summer of 1805. This
watercolour on ivory is by Henry
Bone (1755–1834). (© National
Portrait Gallery, London)

Charles Lamb (1775–1834)
Although Charles Lamb found
Worthing dull, he was inspired
by the names of the inn-keepers
Hogsflesh and Bacon to write a
short comedy called *Mr H*, which
was so bad that it was hissed
when it was first performed
at Drury Lane Theatre in
1806. This 1798 portrait is by
Robert Hancock (1730–1817).
(© National Portrait Gallery,
London)

Don't be envious — Hark what I tell —
You would never do here for a prude,
Because Jack, you know very well,
You were always inclin'd to be rude;

And if you should set up your braying,
And give them but two or three staves,
You would stop all the children from playing,
Or frighten them into the waves!

Sometimes a sick lady will ride me,
More tender and delicate still;
And employ a poor boy just to guide me,
Where I cannot go wrong if I will;

Then back through the town gently creeping,
We stop at some library door;
Where, nonsense preferring to sleeping,
She loads me with novels* a score.

And, dear Jack, by the by, I've long guessed,
Though, good ladies, I've no wish to spite 'em;
That 'tis we bring these books in request,
And that some of our family write 'em.

But who'd go to boast about that?
No, I'll finish by telling you true,
That at Worthing we all might grow fat,
And keep the best company too.

So love to you Jack till next season;
I'll be happy as long as I can;
For an ass that complains without reason,
Becomes — just as bad as a man!

* Every reader will surely know what kind of novels are here alluded to; and, at the same time, truth obliges me to say, that I received personal attentions from Mrs. Spooner, of the Colonade [sic] library, which I remember with gratitude.

Charles Lamb

Charles Lamb, who, as we have seen, knew Robert Bloomfield slightly, is today best remembered for his *Essays of Elia* and the classic children's book *Tales from Shakespeare*, first published in 1807, which he co-wrote with his sister Mary. However Lamb also found literary inspiration in Worthing, and indeed he seems to have visited the town at about the same time as Bloomfield, since the short play that was inspired by his stay was first performed at Drury Lane on 10 December 1806.

Much later Lamb briefly referred to a visit to Worthing in an essay called *The Old Margate Hoy*, which was first published in the *London Magazine* about 1824. However we do not know whether he is describing his original visit or a subsequent one. This is what he wrote:

> I am fond of passing my vacations (I believe I have said so before) at one or other of the Universities. Next to these my choice would fix me at some woody spot, such as the neighbourhood of Henley affords in abundance, upon the banks of my beloved Thames. But somehow or other my cousin contrives to wheedle me once in three or four seasons to a watering place. Old attachments cling to her in spite of experience. We have been dull at Worthing one summer, duller at Brighton another, dullest at Eastbourn [*sic*] a third, and are at this moment doing dreary penance at Hastings! And all because we were happy many years ago for a brief week at Margate.

Dull though he may have found Worthing, Lamb did take one thing away from the visit he paid in 1805 or 1806. This was a delight in the names of the men who, at the start of the nineteenth century, were the landlords of the inns that stood opposite each other at the sea-end of South Street: Hogsflesh at the Sea House Inn and Bacon at the New Inn.

We say 'men', but there is contradiction in the historical record. The newspaper report of 18 August 1805 quoted in Chapter 6 referred to the 'houses' of Mr Hogsflesh and Mr Bacon. John Evans, however, who had visited Worthing in July 1804 and was writing *A Picture of Worthing* later that year, refers to the two inns in question as being 'kept by two widows of the names of Hogsflesh and Bacon'.[3] We know that Thomas Hogsflesh had owned the Sea House Inn from 1786 or earlier, and that Richard Bacon was the landlord of the New Inn by 1792,[4] but the evidence as to when – or indeed in the case of Mrs Bacon, if – their widows took over remains uncertain. John Mackoull, writing in the 1813 edition of *A Sketch of Worthing*, tells us that by that year the inns were run respectively by Mr Parsons and Mr Barker, and confirms that after Hogsflesh died he was briefly succeeded by his widow. However he makes no mention of Bacon's widow in relation to the New Inn, saying only that it was 'late [recently] in the occupation of Mr Bacon'. It may therefore be that Mrs Bacon was never its landlady.

Mackoull claims that 'a singular coincidence of names once occurred' at the New Inn, when Bacon held a dinner party attended not only by Hogsflesh, but also by Mr Wildboar, Mr Swine and Mr Ham. While it is just possible that Bacon assembled such a party to amuse himself and the others, it is more likely that this was a hoary tale that circulated in Worthing, or an invention of Mackoull's.

Either way, Charles Lamb was sufficiently inspired by the names of the two Worthing publicans to use their names in a short two-act comedy with the title of *Mr H*.

The play centres round the main character's being at pains to disguise the fact that his name is Hogsflesh, particularly from Melesinda, the beautiful young woman he hopes to marry. He therefore calls himself Mr H wherever he goes. At the start of the play's second act, however, he accidentally lets slip his real name. Melesinda faints, and it is immediately clear that she will not now go ahead with the marriage.

Terrible pig puns then occupy much of the rest of the play. In the extract that follows, Hogsflesh is exposed to the laboured witticisms of Pry, the landlord of the inn where much of the play is set:

> LANDLORD: Your Honour has had some mortification, to be sure, as a man may say; you have brought your pigs to a fine market.
> MR H: Pigs!
> LANDLORD: What then? Take old Pry's advice, and never mind it. Don't scorch your crackling for 'em, Sir.
> MR H: Scorch my crackling! A queer phrase; but I suppose he don't mean to affront me.

LANDLORD: What is done can't be undone; you can't make a silken purse out of a sow's ear.

MR H: As you say, Landlord, thinking of a thing does but augment it.

LANDLORD: Does but hogment it, indeed, Sir.

MR H: 'Hogment it!' Damn it, I said, 'Augment it.'

LANDLORD: Lord, Sir, 'tis not every body has such gift of fine phrases as your Honour, that can lard his discourse.

MR H: Lard!

LANDLORD: Suppose they do smoke you...

MR H: Smoke me?

LANDLORD: One of my phrases; never mind my words, Sir, my meaning is good. We all mean the same thing, only you express yourself one way, and I another, that's all. The meaning's the same; it is all pork.

The awful pig jokes continue in the next and final scene, which begins with Melesinda's maid, Betty, attempting unsuccessfully to persuade her mistress that a man's name should not matter. But fortunately Hogsflesh has the last laugh – in truth, almost certainly the only laugh – when at the end of the play his old school-friend Belvil produces a newspaper that includes the following item:

The King has been graciously pleased to grant unto John Hogsflesh, Esq., of Sty Hall in the County of Hants, his royal licence and authority that he and his issue may take and use the surname and arms of Bacon in pursuance of an injunction contained in the last will and testament of Nicholas Bacon, Esq. his late uncle, as well as out of grateful respect to his memory, according to the laws of arms, and recorded in the Herald's Office.

The obstacle to Hogsflesh's marriage has been removed, since Melesinda has no objection to being married to a man called Bacon, and the play ends happily. The central character breaks into a short piece of verse, which concludes with the lines: 'For once you've been mistaken / Your shafts have miss'd their aim – Hogsflesh has saved his Bacon.'

(There is a strange pre-echo here of the ending of Oscar Wilde's *The Importance of Being Earnest* – written in Worthing in August and September 1894 – where the obstacle to Jack Worthing's being married to Gwendolen Fairfax is removed when it turns out that his real name is Ernest.)

Unsurprisingly, Lamb's dreadful little play was badly received at Drury Lane Theatre when it was first performed there in 1806. Lamb himself was seated in the pit, and he described the audience reaction in a letter to his friend Thomas Manning over a year later, in February 1808:

Hang 'em, how they hissed! It was not a hiss neither, but a sort of frantic yell, like a congregation of mad geese, with roaring sometimes like bears, mows [grimaces] and mops [pouts] like apes, sometimes snakes, that hissed me into madness.

Lamb apparently also told friends that he joined in the hissing himself, because he was 'so damnably afraid of being taken for the author'.

Although, wisely, Lamb never attempted to write another play, *Mr H* was moderately successful in America, and many years later, on 27 July 1822, it was performed for the first time in Worthing, perhaps partly in tribute to the circumstances in which it had been conceived some sixteen years earlier. It came at the end of one of the multiple bills characteristic of the period. The evening began with a comedy called *The Poor Gentleman*, followed by a solo dance by Miss Smith, a 'favourite song' by Miss Cubitt and a 'comic song' by Mr Burton. Next came a 'laughable interlude' called *The Actress of All Work*, in which almost all the parts were played by Mrs Orger; and the fun-filled evening ended with *Mr H*, on this occasion advertised as *Mister H*. There was a further performance of *Mr H* on 21 August, its title this time printed correctly on the playbill. Most of the rest of the programme was different from that of the previous month, the main attraction this time being a comic opera called *The Foundling of the Forest*. However Miss Smith again danced her dance, and Mr Burton again sang a comic song.

Those behind the production, which was on tour from the Theatre Royal English Opera House, were Benson Earle Hill and his sister Isabel, who had revised the play for its revival. In a book of theatrical reminiscences he published nearly twenty years later, Hill claims that, after the play was performed in Worthing, the local inn-keepers Bacon and Hogsflesh were so dismayed to learn that their names had been mocked on the stage that they called on Trotter to ask 'what they had ever done that a farce should be written purposely to make them the laughing-stocks of the place'. According to Hill, Trotter assured them that its author had never heard of either of them and that he 'bore no malice towards the Swine'. The swine then left mollified, and indeed agreed to see the play if it was ever again performed in Worthing.[5] This anecdote, however, is clearly pure invention on the part of Hill, since, as we have seen, by 1822 Hogsflesh had been dead for at least ten years, and Bacon, if not dead also, had certainly long ago retired from managing the New Inn.

Inevitably Hill adds a few pig puns of his own to his account of these matters, but inexplicably he fails to make anything of the fact that it was a man called Trotter that was the manager under whom this porcine play was performed in Worthing. In now pointing this out, we are pleased to compensate for an omission of almost two centuries.

Lord Byron

Between August 1821 and April 1822 Lord Byron and Percy Bysshe Shelley – fellow-poets and close friends – lived in the same street in Pisa in Italy, Shelley with his second wife Mary, the author of *Frankenstein*; and during this period the two households were in almost constant association with each other.

Byron's company was always entertaining and stimulating, but Shelley found that proximity to his fellow-poet prevented him from writing, and in May 1822 he wrote to his friend Horace Smith: 'I have lived too long near Lord Byron, & the sun has extinguished the glowworm.'

This letter links three notable figures who all visited Worthing in Jane Austen's era, albeit separately and some years apart.

The first to visit was Byron, who was briefly in the town in the summer of 1806.

Byron was the polar opposite of his near-contemporary Jane Austen (she was twelve years older). He was unpredictable, rash, adventurous, and sexually promiscuous with both women and boys. Indeed at the time of his visit to Worthing the love of his life – albeit in this case almost certainly platonic – was a sixteen-year-old Cambridge chorister called John Edleston.

Byron and Jane Austen never met, and there is only one reference in Jane Austen's letters to his poetry. On 5 March 1814 she wrote to Cassandra: 'Do not be angry with me for beginning another Letter to you. I have read the Corsair, mended my petticoat, & have nothing else to do.'

Jane Austen's tone is characteristically light, and nothing should be read into the lack of comment on Byron's *The Corsair*. The fact that Jane Austen read to the end of this long narrative poem – it is over 2,000 lines long – suggests that she found it of interest, and indeed it has recently been argued that Jane Austen 'engaged closely with Byron's poetry and drew inspiration from some of his most popular poems', and that the heroes of *Persuasion* and *Pride and Prejudice* have strong Byronic characteristics.[6]

Theatre Royal, Worthing.

On *WEDNESDAY* Evening, *AUGUST* 21st, 1822,

His Majesty's Servants will perform the Operatic Play of THE

Foundling

Of the Forest.

Count de Valmont ... Mr. TROTTER,   Florian ... ... Mr. HILL,
Baron Longueville ... Mr. THOMPSON,   Bertrand ... Mr. VINING,   L'Eclair ... Mr. BURTON,
Gaspard ... Mr. AYLIFFE,   Sanguine ... Mr. SCOTT,   Lenoir ... Mr. BRINDALL.
Geraldine ... Mrs. FAWCETT,   Rosabelle ... Miss CUBITT,
Monica ... ... Mrs. WILLMOTT,   Eugenia ... ... Mrs. VINING.

In Act the Second,

A PAS SEUL BY MISS J. SMITH.
End of the Play, a Song by Mr. Howard.

After which, the favourite Interlude of

Is he Jealous?

Mr. Belmour ... ... Mr. VINING,
Harriet   Mrs. ORGER,   Mrs. Belmour ... Mrs. FAWCETT,   Rose ... Miss CUBITT.

A COMIC SONG BY MR. BURTON.

To conclude with the Farce of

Mr. H ... ... Mr. HILL,   Belvil ... ... Mr. HOWARD,
Landlord Pry ... Mr. AYLIFFE,   Waiter ... Mr. BRINDALL,   Footman ... Mr. SCOTT.
Melesinda ... Miss CUBITT,   Maid ... ... Mrs. FAWCETT,
Ladies ... ... Mesdames WILLMOTT, WILLIAMS, SMITH, and J. SMITH.

On FRIDAY, " LAUGH WHEN YOU CAN,"
With " *The Lady and the Devil.*"
BY DESIRE AND UNDER THE PATRONAGE OF
The Right Hon. Lady Ossulston.
On SATURDAY,
The Comedy of " ERRORS."

☞ *Tickets and Places for the Boxes may be had of* Mr. RAE, *at the Box-Office of the Theatre from TEN till FOUR o'Clock only.*
LOWER DRESS BOXES, 5s.   UPPER BOXES, 4s.   PIT, 2s. 6d.   GALLERY, 1s.
Evenings of performing, MONDAY, WEDNESDAY, FRIDAY, and SATURDAY.
Doors to be open at a quarter past SIX, and to begin at a quarter past SEVEN precisely.----Half-price to commence
at a quarter past NINE o'Clock.
Second Price to the Boxes, 3s.   Upper Boxes, 2s. 6d.   Pit, 1s. 6d.   Gallery, 6d.
Children under Eight Years of Age to the Boxes, 3s.   Pit, 1s. 6d.
PRIVATE BOXES BY THE NIGHT, WEEK, MONTH, OR SEASON.

CLEMENTS, PRINTER & STATIONER, 9, SOUTH-STREET, WORTHING.

Mr H Comes to Worthing

Charles Lamb's short Worthing-inspired comedy, *Mr H*, first produced in London in 1806, was not performed in Worthing until a touring production visited the town on 27 July 1822 and again on 21 August.

Lord Byron (1788–1824)
Lord Byron stayed briefly in Worthing in August 1806, before joining his friend Edward Long in
Littlehampton. This portrait by Henry Meyer (*c.* 1782–1847), after James Holmes (1777–1860), dates
from 1818. (© National Portrait Gallery, London)

In the summer of 1806 Byron was eighteen years old, and had just completed his first year at Trinity College, Cambridge. In July and early August he had spent three weeks at his mother's house in Southwell in Nottinghamshire, fleeing back to his London lodgings on 7 August after a serious quarrel with her. To his amazement, she followed him to London, and they again had a terrible row about the state of his life and his finances (he was badly in debt to money-lenders). However Byron saw himself as the victor, as he reported in a letter to his Nottinghamshire friend John Pigot on 16 August, in which he also announces that he is about to go to Worthing:

> Mrs. B. returns immediately [to Southwell], but I proceed, with all my laurels, to Worthing, on the Sussex coast; to which place you will address (to be left at the post office) your next epistle. … My stay at Worthing will not exceed three weeks, and you may possibly behold me again at Southwell the middle of September.

Two days later, on 18 August, Byron's departure for Worthing is imminent, but he is much exercised about a lazy and disobedient servant called Charles:

> I am just on the point of setting off for Worthing, and write merely to request you will send that idle scoundrel Charles with my horses immediately; tell him I am excessively provoked he has not made his appearance before, or written to inform me of the cause of his delay, particularly as I supplied him with money for his journey. On no pretext is he to postpone his march one day longer; and if, in obedience to the caprices of Mrs. B. (who, I presume, is again spreading desolation through her little monarchy), he thinks proper to disregard my positive orders, I shall not, in future, consider him as my servant … I delegate to you the unpleasant task of despatching him on his journey – Mrs. B.'s orders to the contrary are not to be attended to: he is to proceed first to London, and then to Worthing, without delay.

The next letter to Pigot is from Littlehampton on 26 August 1806. Again the letter is animated and high-spirited. Although still chiefly occupied with the failings of his servant and his fractious relationship with his mother, he also has good news of a financial nature to pass on:

> I this morning received your epistle, which I was obliged to send for to Worthing, whence I have removed to this place, on the same coast, about eight miles distant from the former. You will probably not be displeased with this letter, when it informs you that I am £30,000 richer than I was at our parting, having just received intelligence from my lawyer that a cause has been gained at Lancaster assizes, which will be worth that sum by the time I come of age. Mrs. B. is, doubtless, acquainted of this acquisition, though not apprised of its exact value of which she had better be ignorant; for her behaviour under any sudden piece of favourable intelligence, is, if possible, more ridiculous than her detestable conduct on the most trifling circumstances of an unpleasant nature. You may give my compliments to her, and say that her detaining my servant's things shall only lengthen my absence: for unless they are immediately despatched to 16, Piccadilly, together with those which have been so long delayed, belonging to myself, she shall never again behold my radiant countenance illuminating her gloomy mansion. If they are sent, I may probably appear in less than two years from the date of my present epistle.[7]

Byron had come to Sussex to join his Cambridge friend, Edward Long, and the reason that he stayed only briefly in Worthing was that the Long and his family turned out in fact to be holidaying in Littlehampton. Edward Long's younger brother, Harry, later wrote a vivid account of Byron's visit.

For some reason Byron stayed at the Dolphin Inn, which Harry describes as 'but a poor place in a dirty village' – it is still a hotel today – rather than the Beach House Hotel, which Harry would have considered more appropriate. Byron had his horses with him, and his adored dog Boatswain (a Newfoundland, the same breed of dog as Edward Ogle owned, as we saw in Chapter 2), who, to Byron's great distress, died two years later after contracting rabies. Byron wrote a poem in Boatswain's memory and built him a marble tomb, which still stands today, in the garden of Newstead Abbey, Byron's ancestral home near Mansfield. The inscription includes the famous lines, written by Byron's friend John Cam Hobhouse: 'Near this Spot / are deposited the Remains of one / Who possessed Beauty Without Vanity / Strength without Insolence / Courage without Ferosity / and all the Virtues of Man without his Vices.'

Byron had also brought his pistols to Littlehampton, and on his first day in the town he amused himself by firing at oyster shells by the pier. Occasionally Byron and Edward Long played cricket on the beach near Mother Zebedees's baths – 'if mere batting and bowling between the two deserves the name' – while the luckless Harry, the sole fielder, had to chase after the ball, with Byron constantly called him 'young shaver'. Byron, a strong swimmer, swam daily in the sea, sometimes carrying Harry on his back. One day Byron and Edward Long foolishly jumped off the end of the pier into the river, and were then carried out to sea by the strong current. It was with some difficulty – and only after 'making an immense semi-circle' – that they were able to swim back to the shore.[8]

Although we have this colourful picture of the young Byron enjoying himself in Littlehampton in the late summer of 1806, we sadly know nothing about his stay in Worthing. However – since it was on 18 August that Byron told Pigot that he was about to leave for Worthing, and it was not until 26 August that he wrote to Pigot from Littlehampton – it is probable that he spent several nights in Worthing before he was able to establish the Longs' correct holiday location.

Non-existent though our knowledge is of what Byron did in Worthing, it is nonetheless pleasing to know that the volatile genius whom his mistress Lady Caroline Lamb famously described as 'mad, bad and dangerous to know' briefly trod the streets of the town less than a year after Jane Austen – who, so far as we are aware, was never accused of being any of those things.

Percy Bysshe Shelley

The pseudonymous poet Paul Potion provides us with our introduction to the Shelley family's connection with Worthing, in these lines from *A Poetical Picture of Worthing and Its Vicinity*:

> Some pleasing woods will here be found,
> And on a spot of rising ground
> A Mansion stands (well worth exploring)
> Of *Sir Bysshe Shelley's* — *Castle Goring*:
> Who has a son nam'd *Timothy*
> And of New Shoreham too — M.P.!

Castle Goring was built by Shelley's grandfather, Bysshe (later Sir Bysshe) Shelley, and was intended to become the Shelley family seat. However Sir Bysshe never seems to have occupied the house, and towards the end of his life – he died in 1815 – preferred to live in a small cottage in Horsham near his favourite tavern. Similarly the poet's father, Timothy, had no desire to move from Field Place, near Horsham, where the poet was born in 1792.

Percy Shelley would, however, have become the owner – and perhaps the occupant – of

Percy Bysshe Shelley (1792–1822)
Shelley's family were landowners in and around Worthing, and his grandfather Bysshe (later Sir Bysshe)
Shelley built Castle Goring. Shelley's first two books were printed in Worthing in 1810–11. This
portrait by Amelia Curran (1775–1847) dates from 1819. (© National Portrait Gallery, London)

Montague Place

In the first of these three watercolours of 1813 the prominent building at centre-left is Montpelier Terrace, which dated from *c.* 1810 and was demolished in 1975. To its right is Montague Terrace, which still stands. The house at centre-right is Sumner Lodge, later called Summer House.

East from Montpelier Terrace

On the left is the corner of Montpelier Terrace, followed by Sumner Lodge. At centre-right is Bath Buildings. There was no promenade along the shore at Worthing until the Esplanade was completed in 1821, so houses and gardens gave straight onto the beach.

The Steyne

This view shows, left to centre right: Steyne Hotel, Steyne Row (with a gap in the middle, as now) and the Colonnade. Warwick House is hidden among the trees. On the right of the picture is Greville (later Gravel) Terrace, which still stands today.

Castle Goring had he not died young, drowning in Lake Geneva in 1822, a few weeks before his thirtieth birthday. But Shelley has another connection with Worthing, and one that is much better documented than his friend Byron's.

Shelley had become a student at University College, Oxford in April 1810, and in late 1810 and early 1811 his first two books were printed in Worthing. Presumably he sometimes stayed at Castle Goring, since that is the only logical explanation for its having been a Worthing firm that he used. Indeed, oddly, the firm in question also had premises in Horsham, conveniently located for Field Place, Shelley's father's house. It was from the Horsham premises that James Phillips printed the early playbills for the Worthing theatre, and it was probably this connection that in 1810 led Phillips to open a branch in Worthing, at 12 Warwick Street (now, after renumbering, No. 23), which was run by his sons Charles and William.

The member of the firm most actively involved in preparing Shelley's books was an intelligent and personable young woman called Miss Phillips – her first name is not known – who was either the sister or the cousin of Charles and William. Shelley seems to have taken a great interest in printing procedures and processes, and often went to 12 Warwick Street to watch and assist. But apparently another reason for the regularity of his visits was that he found the beguiling Miss Phillips of as much interest as the printing. Shelley – who had turned eighteen on 4 August, and so was the same age as Byron had been when he visited Worthing four years earlier – was almost as susceptible to the charms of attractive young women as his friend notoriously was.[9]

Both the books that Shelley arranged to be printed in Worthing were to prove controversial. The first, *Original Poetry by Victor and Cazire*, published in September 1810, was a collection of poems by Shelley and his sister Elizabeth. All but three or four of the poems were Shelley's, and his poems were indeed original – but one of Elizabeth's was not. It was quickly discovered that one of her contributions was a straight copy of a poem by the famous Gothic writer 'Monk' Lewis. When Shelley found out, he was furious, and he had no alternative but to order that all the copies of the book that had not yet been distributed should be destroyed.

However this was as nothing to the trouble caused by the second publication. This was a pamphlet with the self-explanatory title *The Necessity of Atheism*, which was published in February 1811. Promoting atheism was regarded as blasphemy, and was therefore an offence against common law, and C. & W. Phillips could have been prosecuted. Nonetheless Shelley unwisely arranged for his book to be sold in a bookshop in Oxford, where a senior figure in the university saw it and drew the bookseller's attention to its pernicious nature, whereupon all the copies were burnt.

The trail then quickly led to Shelley, who was summoned in front of the authorities at University College and asked if he had written it. He refused to answer, and was immediately expelled. His friend Thomas Jefferson Hogg, who had helped Shelley with the book, wrote to the college authorities to object to Shelley's expulsion, whereupon he was expelled also. Shelley's father managed to persuade University College to agree to reinstate his son on condition that he abandoned his atheistic views, but Shelley refused to do so, and this led to a falling-out with his father. Their relationship deteriorated still further four months later when Shelley, still only nineteen, eloped to Scotland with the sixteen-year-old Harriet Westbrook, whom his father regarded as both too young and socially inferior. Shelley's relationship with his father never recovered from these events.

There is no evidence that Shelley ever returned to Worthing, and indeed much of the rest of his life was spent abroad. In August 1826, however, four years after her husband's death, Shelley's second wife Mary paid a visit to Castle Goring to see the estate which their son, also Percy (1819–89), would in due course inherit. Then in 1844, on his grandfather's death, the younger Percy duly became the 3rd Baronet of Castle Goring. He toyed with the idea of living there, but to furnish and maintain this large house proved beyond his means, and it was sold the following year.[10]

Horace Smith

Our next visitor to early Worthing is Shelley's close friend Horace Smith. Horace Smith – sometimes known as Horatio, the name by which he was christened – was an unusual combination: a successful stockbroker, and a distinguished poet and novelist. He helped Shelley manage his finances and interceded with Shelley's father when he withdrew Shelley's allowance. Shelley thought highly of Smith, once saying of him: 'Is it not odd that the only truly generous person I ever knew, who had money to be generous with, should be a stockbroker! And he writes poetry too.'[11]

Smith had a poetic connection with both Byron and Shelley. In the case of Byron, this relates to a very popular book of parodies of the best-known poets of the time that Horace Smith and his brother James published in 1812 under the title *Rejected Addresses: Or, The New Theatrum Poetarum*. The parody of Byron's poetry was the work of Horace, and it was so clever that Byron said that he found it difficult to believe that he had not written the verse himself.

We know that Jane Austen was also a great admirer of the Smith brothers' parodies, for in a letter of 24 January 1813 she tells Cassandra how much she has enjoyed a book by Captain Pasley called *Essay on the Military Police & Institutions of the British Empire*, then adding: 'I am as much in love with the Author as I ever was with Clarkson or Buchanan, or even the two Mr Smiths of the city.'

Horace Smith's connection with Shelley's poetry is of particular interest. Early in 1818 Shelley and Smith, in friendly rivalry, published competing sonnets on the same theme in, respectively, the January and February editions of a journal called *The Examiner*. That theme was the story of Ozymandias. Smith's sonnet is an accomplished piece of verse, but it was eclipsed by Shelley's, which has become one of the best-loved poems in the English language.

Smith was, as it happens, on his way to join Shelley in Italy when he was informed in Paris of the poet's death,[12] and it is perhaps not a coincidence that he should have visited Worthing two and a half months later, in September 1822, since, as we have seen, Smith had some involvement in Shelley's financial affairs. The main purpose of the visit may therefore have been to attend to matters relating to Shelley's estate. Whatever the reason for his stay, Smith turned his experiences in the town into a satirical narrative.

Smith's satire – entitled *Select Society; or, a Week at Worthing*, and first published in the *New Monthly Magazine* in 1822[13] – is the most vivid account we have of Worthing during the period covered by this book, and it paints a delightful and atmospheric picture of a town whose character was still much as it had been when Jane Austen visited in 1805. Extra immediacy is generated by the fact that Smith mentions so many Worthing locations by name.

It must, however, be borne in mind that Smith is writing not as himself, but 'in character' as an aspirational lower-middle-class grocer from Tooley Street in London. (Tooley Street is just south of the Thames, between London Bridge and Tower Bridge and thus, coincidentally, almost opposite where the Ogle brothers' wharf was located.) While it is difficult to avoid the conclusion that Smith himself found Worthing dull, his gentle satire, written in the form of a sequence of diary entries, is directed just as much at his narrator as at the town – since part of the reason that the narrator is bored by Worthing is that he has little interest in anything unfamiliar and hates being away from London. Nonetheless, Smith presents his narrator as amiable and warm-hearted – unlike the members of 'select society', whose lack of courtesy is a recurring theme.

Horace Smith (1779–1849)
Horace Smith, christened Horatio Smith, was a stockbroker and a poet and critic. His satirical piece *Select Society; or, a Week at Worthing*, first published in the *New Monthly Magazine* in 1822, gives a vivid picture of Worthing in the early years of the nineteenth century.

The Royal Baths and Marlborough House
This building, part baths and part hotel, was built for and owned by Thomas Trotter, the manager of the Theatre Royal, and designed by John Rebecca, the architect of many of Worthing's finest early buildings, including Castle Goring and the Chapel of Ease. It was built about 1818 and demolished in 1940. At the time of Horace Smith's and Colonel Berkeley's visits, Trotter's baths would have been the best in Worthing, with Wicks's Warm Baths (see pictures on pages 37 and 89) by then rather old-fashioned.

While the anecdotes and encounters in the 'diary' may be rooted in the reality of a visit that Smith undoubtedly did pay to Worthing in September 1822 – as we shall see, there are references to plays that were performed at Worthing's theatre during that month – the tale is much embellished for humorous effect, and many of the characters are clearly imaginary, with fanciful names of the type that feature in the comic plays of the period.

The narrator's reason for going to Worthing, as he tells his friend Tom Turpentine on the day he travels down to Sussex, is that he has heard how 'select' the society in the town is and wants to become part of it. The attempt, however, is a failure, and the piece ends with the narrator, on his return to London, sending Turpentine a note that reads: 'No more weeks at Worthing! Select society is all very well for select people.'

Shortly after Smith's narrator arrives in Worthing, on the afternoon of Monday 2 September, he sets eyes on the sea for the first time in his life, and is unimpressed:

> Arrived at Worthing at half past four. Head dizzy with the rattling of coach steps. Steyne Hotel: ordered a veal cutlet at five, and walked out to view the ocean. Never saw it before, and never

more disappointed. Expected waves mountains high, shrieking mariners, swamped long-boat, 'and all that sort of thing'. Smooth as West India docks. Walked up to Wick's [*sic*] warm baths.

The narrator then sees a playbill advertising that evening's offering, *Cure for the Heartache*, due to begin at seven. He looks at his watch, and is surprised to find that it is still only six, so he takes a stroll five times up and down Ann Street to pass the time until the play starts. The part of Young Rapid in *Cure for the Heartache* is taken by the theatre's 'tall manager'. (This was the Theatre Royal's actor-manager, Thomas Trotter, of whom we read in Chapter 6.)

On Tuesday the narrator spends some time looking through a telescope; discovers that the town's bathing machines are available only for men; and pays seven and sixpence to join Stafford's Library, where he reads a newspaper. He then dines upon 'fried soles', which 'tasted too much of the sea'. In the evening he returns to the library in search of entertainment, but finds it 'dull and cold'. A girl in pink plays a piece called *We're a' Noddin*, and the narrator observes: 'Sure enough we all were.'

On Wednesday he goes to see the famous Miller's Tomb on Highdown Hill – and thinks little of it, pointing out that there are the tombs of three millers in St George's churchyard in Southwark. In the evening he wanders out onto the seafront and casts 'a longing look towards Brighton' through a telescope. He goes to see a play called *Honey Moon*, which features a celebrated actress called Miss Dance 'for that night only'. He finds her 'too lady-like' for the part. After the play he returns to the beach and spends half-an-hour watching 'a lighter [flat-bottomed boat] discharge coals by candle-light'. Then he goes to bed and dreams of Miss Dance.

On Thursday he tries a bathing machine, an experience he does not enjoy. Afterwards he hires a donkey cart to take him to Chanctonbury Ring. In the evening he goes again to the library, where the entertainment is provided by the same girl as on Tuesday – she is, it now appears, a harpist – and with the same result: 'All nodding again.'

On Friday morning the tide is low, and everyone is promenading on the beach, where Smith's narrator encounters two members of 'select society', General Culverin and Lady Seraphina Surf. He pats Lady Seraphina's poodle, saying 'What a beauty!', but she and the general ride off without saying anything to him. He decides that select society is 'rather rude' and wonders whether 'a touch of vulgarity would not make it more polite'. As on other days, time hangs heavy; and he longs to be back in London:

Looked at my watch, and wondered it was only twelve. Strolled up Steyne-row into the town. Stopped at the corner of Warwick-street, and looked into a grocer's shop. Had half a mind to borrow a white apron, and offer to serve behind the counter to keep my hand in … Recollected I was a gentleman, and sighed. Took a walk on the Lancing-road. Met some gypsies, who told my fortune. Said I should be in a great place shortly. Told them I hoped I should, and that I was a fool for ever quitting it.

In the evening he goes to the theatre again. He does not name the play, only telling us that it is sponsored by Lady Longshore, whose name appears in large print at the top of the posters.

Saturday is Market Day, so the narrator 'spent two hours in seeing the women spread their crockery upon the pavement'. He decides to visit Caesar's Camp, which he has overheard Lady Seraphina and two other members of the nobility discussing. (This was Cissbury Ring – it used to be thought that Cissbury meant 'Caesar's fort'.) Having not enjoyed the donkey-cart ride to Chanctonbury on Thursday, he this time hires a pony-chaise from a stand opposite Wicks's Warm Baths. He finds the pony-chaise 'quite genteel', but Caesar's Camp is a disappointment. He had expected Caesar still to be there and to hear drums and fifes, but instead he finds 'nothing but mounds of earth and thistles'. It is clear to him that 'General Caesar' has decamped – 'and I dare say in debt to half the town'. In the evening he goes to the theatre to see *Romeo and Juliet*, and then returns to his hotel room and reads the *Brighton Herald*, which makes him wish he was in Brighton. After that he distracts himself by poring over a map of Sussex; counting the knobs on the fender; and reading a copy of the Army List.

(Playbills and other records for the Theatre Royal, Worthing from September 1822[14] confirm that the plays attended by the narrator were indeed performed there during that month, but curiously the dates do not cohere. In small towns such as Worthing in those days plays generally ran for one night only, and *A Cure for the Heartache* was performed not on Monday 2 September but on Saturday 7 September. *Honey Moon*, the play starring Miss Dance, was performed not on Wednesday 4 September but on Friday 13 September, this indeed being Miss Dance's 'first and only appearance' in Worthing. *Romeo and Juliet*, 'not acted these seven years' – and incongruously featuring Thomas Trotter, then aged forty-three, as an over-ripe Romeo – was performed on Saturday 14 September, and was not repeated that season. These dates suggest that Smith's real visit was from about 7 to 15 September, the week after his fictional narrator's.[15])

Sunday is the dullest day yet. The narrator goes to a service at the Chapel of Ease. He had intended to put just a shilling in the collection at the end, but since the ubiquitous Lady Seraphina is holding the plate he feels obliged to give half a crown instead. She fails to thank him, and his opinion of select society declines still further. He cannot face the thought of going into the town, since both the billiard-room and the library are closed on Sundays. Instead he strolls to Broadwater Common and amuses himself by picking blackberries – something that this Londoner has evidently never done before, since his method is to break off a large branch, which he takes this back to Worthing 'in triumph' and gives to a child 'at the corner of South-street'. He then walks on the beach and throws a stone six feet away from him – followed by a further ninety-nine in an attempt to hit it. He yawns heavily, and soon his mouth is constantly wide open from yawning. He is therefore much relieved, on dining at five, to find that he is still able to close it in order to chew his food.

On Monday it is with great relief that Smith's narrator mounts Newman's patent safety-coach and leaves Worthing. He feels very ill at the start of the journey, but he recovers as he approaches 'wholesome London air'; and he sniffs 'the breezes of Bermondsey with peculiar satisfaction'.

The most characteristic moment in Smith's charming satirical piece comes in a brief conversation that takes place on the day his narrator goes to Chanctonbury Hill.

The driver of the donkey cart tells the narrator that the view from Chanctonbury is the finest in the world.

'How much of the world have you seen?'

'Lancing, Shoreham, and Broadwater Green,' the man replies.

Colonel Berkeley and Mrs Bunn

The cartoon on the facing page, depicting a scene that the milestone tells us is supposed to be four miles from Worthing, was first published in August 1825. Although the complicated but fascinating story behind it will take us to various other locations, the Worthing connection is strong enough to justify its being told here. In addition, it will give a vivid picture of an England that was very different from the decorous world of Jane Austen's novels, and fleshes out for us the underbelly of – to use Horace Smith's phrase – the 'select society' of the time.[16]

The man in the picture is Colonel Berkeley, who – among many other things – was an enthusiastic amateur actor. The woman is the well-known actress Mrs Bunn. It was a theatrical commitment that brought them to Worthing in the summer of 1825, at a time when Colonel Berkeley's name was engulfed in a succession of scandals that caused a combination of amusement and moral outrage to the newspaper readers of the time.

The maiden name of Mrs Bunn, who was born in 1799, was Margaret Somerville. She became Mrs Bunn on her marriage in 1819 to Alfred Bunn, 'a little gentleman of excessive irascibility' who was intermittently a successful theatre manager, for many years in charge of Covent Garden Theatre and later the Drury Lane Theatre. A young woman of great beauty – she was twenty-five at the time of her appearance in Worthing – Mrs Bunn was regarded in some quarters as one of the best tragic heroines of her day, although one critic described her Lady Macbeth as 'even more monotonous than a church spout when it pours in wet weather' and the great actor Edmund Kean, who was less than five feet seven inches tall, tried to avoid acting with her because he said she was 'too big and o'ertowering a woman' for his small figure.[17]

Colonel Berkeley – William Fitzhardinge Berkeley (1786–1857) – was the illegitimate son of the 5th Earl of Berkeley by his mistress, the daughter of a publican and butcher. The earl subsequently married William's mother, in 1796, but he also claimed there had been an earlier marriage ceremony, in 1785, and William therefore grew up believing that he would inherit his father's title. After his father died in 1810, however, the House of Lords decided that there was

Colonel Berkeley and Mrs Bunn on the Road to Worthing
This cartoon implies not only that Colonel Berkeley was having an affair with the actress Mrs Bunn at the time that the two of them were performing at the Theatre Royal in Worthing but also that he was paying her husband Alfred Bunn for the privilege. The identities of the two characters are shown by the signpost on the right, one arm of which reads 'To Berkely [*sic*] Square' and the other 'To Bunhill Row'. The artist is Robert Cruikshank (1789–1856), elder brother of Charles Dickens's illustrator, George Cruikshank. (© British Museum)

no satisfactory proof of the earlier marriage. Since William was deemed to have been born out of wedlock, he could not accede to the title, and for many years he was known only as Colonel Berkeley. He was, however, able to console himself with the fact that he inherited his father's estates and properties in Gloucestershire, which included Berkeley Castle, famous as the location where King Edward II was murdered in 1327. One day in October 1812 Berkeley entertained there two other figures that appear in this book, Joseph Grimaldi and Lord Byron. Byron played an unkind trick on the naive and good-hearted Grimaldi, prevailing upon him to eat apple tart with soy sauce. Grimaldi did his best to swallow a mouthful of this 'vile mess', and apologised to Byron for being unable to do so, upon which 'the rest of the company laughed most heartily'.[18]

Berkeley was described by an anonymous contemporary observer as 'one of the most repulsive oafs and ruffians in the annals of the peerage' and by the diarist Charles Greville as 'an arrant blackguard … notorious for general worthlessness'. The diarist Harriet Arbuthnot wrote that he was 'a vulgar, narrow-minded man, for his great pleasure seems to be to act the sort of King of Cheltenham, where all the vulgar misses make a great piece of work with him'.[19] (Berkeley was not the first or the last oaf and blackguard to be irresistible to the female sex.)

Berkeley does appear, however, to have been a decent actor. *The Drama, or Theatrical Pocket Magazine*, a monthly journal published in London, includes this in a report of 12 July 1822 about recent performances at the Cheltenham Theatre:

Colonel Berkeley Gives Jasper Judge a Horsewhipping
Accompanied by his friends Lord Sussex Lennox and John Carr Hammond, Colonel Berkeley punishes Jasper Judge for printing disobliging facts about him in the *Cheltenham Journal*. Colonel Berkeley had to take time off from performing at Worthing's Theatre Royal in August 1825 to appear at Hereford assizes in connection with this assault. The artist is again Robert Cruikshank. (© British Museum)

On Thursday, July 4, the house was crowded to excess to witness the representation of *Henri Quatre*, by those amateurs who have so frequently graced the boards of our theatre, and with such well-merited approbation. The part of *Henri* was sustained by Colonel BERKELEY, whose full-toned voice, majestic appearance, and splendid dress, independent of his qualifications as an actor, induced the audience to acknowledge with thunders of applause that he looked and acted '*aye every inch a king*'. Captain AUGUSTUS BERKELEY [Colonel Berkeley's brother] performed *Eugene de Biron*, whose romantic character could not well have found a better representation.

This report – which is signed E. M. – should, however, be treated with a certain amount of caution, since its author was clearly the journal's Cheltenham correspondent and it would have been in his interests to stay on the right side of so powerful a figure in the town as Berkeley. In addition, local reviewers are usually quicker to praise and slower to be critical than their metropolitan counterparts.

In the summer of 1815 Colonel Berkeley became captivated by the beauty of a young actress called Maria Foote. Maria Foote – or Miss Foote, as she was always known, since in those days neither actors nor actresses used their first names – went on to become one of the most celebrated actresses of her day. Indeed when, in 1938, a plaque was placed on the former Worthing theatre (which by then had been a warehouse for over eighty years), she was one of the ten actors and actresses chosen to represent the famous players who had performed there. However her success seems to have owed more to her exceptional beauty – and indeed to the scandal in which she was involved – than to outstanding acting talents.

Maria Foote was born in June 1798[20] and therefore had just turned seventeen when she attracted the attention of Colonel Berkeley, who was by then in his thirties. Colonel Berkeley asked the manager of the Cheltenham Theatre if he could play a role in a benefit performance for her, and the acquaintance he stage-managed in this way soon developed into a relationship. Miss Foote's understanding was always that Berkeley would in due course marry her, and in 1821 she had a child by him and retired from the stage – in the event only temporarily – prompting an anonymous author in the *New Monthly Magazine* (it was possibly Horace Smith) to write:

> Is comedy entirely to lose the most delicate and graceful of its handmaidens, and tragedy the loveliest of its sufferers? ... In return for those images of pure and innocent beauty with which she has enriched our imaginations, we wish her all the good, which should attend one of Nature's choicest favourites.[21]

In the event Miss Foote did return to the stage. There was still no sign of the promised marriage, and in the spring of 1824, by now pregnant with Berkeley's second child, she ended her relationship with him.

One of the reasons for her decision was that the previous year she had acquired another rich admirer, Joseph 'Pea-Green' Hayne, whose nickname (probably bestowed on him by Berkeley) derived from the colour of the coat he habitually wore. 'Pea-Green' Hayne was twenty-three or twenty-four at the time, 'a man of the town, a man of fashion and gaiety' and, importantly, 'possessed of a large independent fortune'.[22] Miss Foote clearly thought him a good match. However he knew nothing of her past, and there was the awkward matter of her second pregnancy to conceal. When this reached the point where it could no longer be disguised, Miss Foote disappeared to the country with her mother until after the child was born.

When in due course Berkeley discovered that 'Pea-Green' Hayne wanted to marry Maria, he told him of his own long association with her and of the fact that she had borne him two children. Hayne, on the one hand besotted and on the other indecisive, kept changing his mind, and he jilted her on no fewer than three occasions. After the final time, Maria sued him for breach of promise, and the case came to court in December 1824. She told the court that she had given Berkeley custody of her two children in anticipation of marrying Hayne, and that she had sold her theatrical wardrobe prior to her retirement from the stage. She asked for £20,000 in damages, but was awarded only £3,000, much of which went on her legal fees.

No less a figure than the Attorney-General represented Miss Foote in court, and he was scathing about Berkeley's behaviour, saying that he 'could not trust himself in using language he thought sufficient to express his detestation of Colonel Berkeley's conduct'. Until the breach of promise case, Colonel Berkeley's long-standing relationship with Maria Foote had been a largely private matter, but now it was universally known, and he was exposed to much unfavourable comment in the newspapers. Particularly virulent in his condemnation of Berkeley was the editor of the *Cheltenham Journal*, a man called Jasper Judge, who printed a story to the effect that he was the illegitimate son of the 5th Earl of Berkeley by a butcher's daughter; that his conduct to Miss Foote was infamous; that he was destitute of courage; and that many respectable people refused to invite him to their hunt balls.

Since everything that Judge wrote was either true or legitimate comment, Berkeley did not have the option of suing for libel. Instead he went to Judge's house on 14 March 1825 with two friends, Lord Sussex Lennox and John Carr Hammond; knocked Judge to the ground; and vigorously set about him with what was later described in court as a 'heavy jockey whip'. When Judge staggered out of the room, streaming with blood from head to foot, Berkeley's friends held him so that Berkeley could continue to horsewhip him. Judge's wig came off, whereupon Berkeley whipped him on his bare head. One of Judge's eyes was damaged, possibly irreparably, and his injuries were so serious that he claimed in court that he had to spend a fortnight in bed.[23]

Berkeley, Hammond and Lennox were duly indicted for the assault, and the case was set down to be heard at Hereford assizes on 4 August 1825.

During the week before the trial – and also during the week after – Berkeley was on stage at the Theatre Royal in Worthing. On the evening of 30 July he played the title role in *Othello*, with Captain Augustus Berkeley as Iago. The 'two gentlemen amateurs' also appeared in *Follies of a Day*, an English translation of *The Marriage of Figaro* by Beaumarchais, today more famous in Mozart's operatic version. Unsurprisingly, Worthing's Theatre Royal was sold out, and indeed tickets for the double-bill exchanged hands at well above face value. The performances by the Berkeleys the week following the trial – these took place on 11, 12 and 13 August — also played to packed houses, although it is not recorded whether the plays were the same as on 30 July.[24]

Mrs Bunn now enters the story, for she played Desdemona in *Othello* and also appeared in *Follies of a Day*. The satirical cartoon reproduced on page 113 that has provided the stimulus for this investigation makes it clear that Berkeley was more than just the theatrical bed-mate of his Desdemona and that he was paying for the privilege.

Berkeley's relationship with Mrs Bunn was also noted elsewhere in the press. On 8 October 1825 the very first issue of *The Spirit of the Times*, a weekly paper that prided itself on 'concentrating all that is worthy of being preserved from the whole of our periodical literature' made mention of their affair. In a gossip column called 'Lost and Found', it included this in the 'Found' category: 'Mrs Bunn and Colonel Berkeley, in the interior of a carriage, while the lady's husband sported the *dickey*.' A footnote at the bottom of the page makes clear that the implication of the final seven words is that Alfred Bunn was being cuckolded.

Further proof that Berkeley was having a relationship with Mrs Bunn at this time came two years later, when the husband of another woman with whom Berkeley had an affair in 1825 sued him for damages, and was awarded £1,000. This was Mrs Dauncey, who may have been the wife of a Gloucestershire barrister of that name who had acted for Berkeley in a notorious case of 1816 involving the murder of one of Berkeley's gamekeepers by a gang of poachers. Berkeley's

Margaret Somerville, later Mrs Bunn (1799–1883)
Margaret Somerville became Mrs Bunn on her marriage in 1819 to the theatre manager Alfred
Bunn, who apparently condoned her relationship with Colonel Berkeley in exchange for money. This
engraving by Frederick Christian Lewis Sr (1779–1856), after Sir George Hayter (1792–1871), dates
from 1816. (© National Portrait Gallery, London)

Maria Foote, later Countess of Harrington (1798–1867)
Maria Foote – who herself appeared at the Theatre Royal in Worthing (three times in August 1830, and almost certainly on other occasions also) – had two children by Colonel Berkeley and was then jilted by the besotted but indecisive Joseph 'Pea-Green' Hayne. In 1831 she retired from the stage to marry Charles Stanhope, 4th Earl of Harrington. This engraving by Charles Picart (*c.*1780–*c.* 1837), after George Clint (1770–1854), dates from 1822. (© National Portrait Gallery, London)

affair with Mrs Dauncey seems to have taken place in the spring and summer of 1825, but by October she had become aware that Mrs Bunn was living with Berkeley at Berkeley Castle. Mrs Dauncey made her feelings clear by asking her sister to go to Berkeley Castle 'dressed as a servant-maid' and deliver a parcel containing some verses and a bun. Mrs Dauncey's sister explained to the court the reason for the bun: 'She told me she sent the bun on account of a Mrs Bunn, who was then staying in the castle.'[25]

(According to the memoirs of one of his younger brothers, Berkeley soon relegated Mrs Bunn to the status of his second-favourite mistress. He installed her in a house in Cheltenham called German Cottage; but soon afterwards 'he hired a lodging in an adjacent street' for his 'first favourite', 'the more notorious Mrs Barker'.[26])

But we return to the summer of 1825, when Berkeley's pleasure in playing to packed houses in Worthing with Mrs Bunn had to be interrupted for him to attend to unfinished business arising from the break-up of his relationship with Maria Foote and his subsequent horsewhipping of Jasper Judge. On 4 August he appeared at Hereford assizes in front of Mr Justice Burrough and a jury. The prosecution counsel, Mr Phillips, outlined the story of Berkeley's assault on Judge in the terms described earlier, while Berkeley's counsel, Mr Taunton, suggested in mitigation that Berkeley had delivered a 'good old English punishment' that was entirely appropriate for the insult he had suffered. In his summing-up, the judge expressed a certain amount of sympathy for Colonel Berkeley, directing the attention of the jury to the great provocation he had received and commenting that it was 'not to be endured' that the press should drag the 'private transactions' of a man's life before the public. However the judge felt that Berkeley had been wrong to take the two others with him when he went to see Jasper Judge. He said that it would have been acceptable if Berkeley had met Judge in the street and 'inflicted a moderate chastisement' on him, but this was not 'a manly horsewhipping'. The judge accordingly instructed the jury to specify the damages they considered appropriate, and Judge was awarded £500.[27]

This was not the final piece of litigation involving Colonel Berkeley in 1825. Interest in his relationship with Miss Foote rumbled on, and in October Berkeley was subjected to such a clear-cut libel that he sued. It appears that 'most of the papers' had printed a story to the effect that 'an unmanly ruffian' had 'secreted himself in Miss Foote's bedchamber, at her hotel, in Edinburgh for some base purpose'. The ruffian in question was certainly not Berkeley, who had not been to Edinburgh for four years and would have had no reason to hide in Miss Foote's hotel bedroom, but a paper called, ironically enough, *Common Sense, or the Weekly Globe*, unwisely added to its report: 'A clue has however been found, for a private correspondent informs us, that this ruffian was no other than Col. Berkeley, in the disguise of a gentleman.' The case came before the courts on 8 November and again on 17 November, on which date the judge asked the publisher of *Common Sense* to provide justification. The final outcome is not known.[28]

Intriguingly the publishers of *Common Sense* were back in court the following day, this time to answer a charge of libel 'of the most malignant description' against Alfred Bunn, whose wife, as we know, was having an affair with Colonel Berkeley at this time. It cannot be a coincidence that these two libel actions were heard in immediate proximity to each other. *The Examiner* reported that *Common Sense* had 'imputed to Mr Bunn an abominable offence, which must exclude any man from society'. The 'abominable offence' is not specified, but it is likely that the paper had suggested that Bunn had condoned Berkeley's affair with his wife in return for money. Bunn was in financial difficulties at the time and, as we have seen, the cartoon reproduced on page 113 indicates that Berkeley paid for the pleasure of Mrs Bunn's company. Bunn's libel case returned to court on 13 June the following year, and resulted in one of the publishers of *Common Sense* being jailed for a month.[29]

Miss Foote's career was not harmed by these sensational legal cases, not least because she was felt to be the – relatively – innocent victim of male mis-treatment by both Berkeley and Hayne. Indeed she was herself at the Theatre Royal in Worthing five years later, on the nights of 25, 26 and 27 August 1830, playing to packed houses, just as Berkeley had done five years earlier. Her name appeared on the playbill at a size that dwarfed all other information, evidence of what a big attraction she had become.[30]

Both Berkeley and Miss Foote later rose to become members of the nobility. Although, as we have seen, Berkeley had been frustrated in 1811 in his desire to become the 6th Earl of Berkeley by benefit of birth, he went to become an earl by creation, his reputation as a bounder and a libertine seemingly proving no barrier to his advancement. In 1831 he was made Lord Seagrave; in 1836 he was appointed Lord-Lieutenant of Gloucestershire (as his father and grandfather had been); and in 1841 he was created Earl Fitzhardinge. The title died with him in 1857, since he never married and therefore had no legitimate children.

Meanwhile Maria Foote became the mistress of Charles Stanhope, 4th Earl of Harrington, an exceptionally handsome man much celebrated for the elegance of his dress, and in 1831 she retired from the stage in order to marry him. The new Countess of Harrington was held in high regard by all who knew her, for she was not only beautiful and charming, but also apparently had much sweetness of character. She died in 1867, ten years after Colonel Berkeley and sixteen years after her husband.

Alfred Bunn died in 1860. Mrs Bunn outlived all the others, dying in Blue Earth City, Minnesota in January 1883, at the age of eighty-three.

Notes

For the convenience of the reader, the full title of a book, the publisher's name and the date of publication are given on its first citation in each chapter, rather than just the first time it is cited in the book. A shorter version is used for subsequent citations in a given chapter.

Robert Elleray's *A Millennium Encyclopaedia of Worthing History* (Optimus, 1998) is nowhere cited in these notes, but this indispensable source of facts and dates relating to Worthing was regularly consulted during the writing of this book.

Introduction: Jane Austen and Early Worthing

1. A. M. Rowland and T. P. Hudson, *The Victoria History of the County of Sussex*, Vol. 6, Part 1 (1980), p. 94.
2. Deirdre Le Faye, ed., *Jane Austen's Letters* (OUP, 2011), p. 259. I am indebted to Deirdre Le Faye for alerting me to this reference to Ogle after she read an early version of my article 'Edward Ogle of Worthing and Jane Austen's Sanditon' prior to its publication in the *Jane Austen Society Report for 2010*.
3. Deirdre Le Faye, *A Chronology of Jane Austen and her Family* (Cambridge University Press, 2006), p. 586.
4. Janet Sanders, 'Sanditon', *Times Literary Supplement*, 19 February 1925, p. 120.
5. Jane Austen's niece Anna Lefroy refers to the work as *Sanditon* in a family letter of 1869. See Kathryn Sutherland, ed., *A Memoir of Jane Austen* (Oxford University Press, 2002), p. 184.
6. Information from www.measuringworth.com

Chapter 1: Warwick House – The Model for 'Trafalgar House'

1. Where no other source reference is given, the information in this chapter mostly derives from Henfrey Smail, *Warwick House* (Aldridge Bros, 1952) or, in a few cases, from Henfrey Smail, *The Worthing Map Story* (Aldridge Bros, 1949).
2. *Stafford's Guide to Worthing* (1810) quoted in Various, *The Worthing Parade, Number Two* (Aldridge Bros, 1954), p. 38.
3. *The Worthing Parade, Number Two*, pp. 38–39.
4. John Evans, *A Picture of Worthing* (C. Stower, 1805), p. 17.
5. Thomas Yeakell & William Gardner, *A Topographical Survey of the County of Sussex* (1778–83), cited on p. 97 of A. M. Rowland and T. P. Hudson, *The Victoria History of the County of Sussex*, Vol. 6, Part 1 (1980). *The Topographer for the Year 1791* (J. Robson & others, 1791), Vol. 4, p. 149, does not give a date for the house, referring only to the 'pleasant hamlet of Worthing ... where the Earl of Warwick has purchased a good house'.
6. National Archives, Add Mss 46180 & 46181, 21 August 1795.
7. National Archives, Add Mss 46183 & 46184, 24 & 25 March 1801.
8. John Shearsmith, *A Topographical Description of Worthing* (G. Verrall, 1824), pp. 14–15.
9. The name Potion suggests someone in the medical profession, so a possible candidate for the poem's authorship is John Shearsmith, who was a doctor in Worthing at the time.
10. Paul Potion, *A Poetical Picture of Worthing and Its Vicinity* (W. Phillips, 1814), pp. 28–9. Potion spells Claude Lorraine's surname incorrectly.
11. Sale document relating to the auction on 12 June 1888, cited in Smail, *Warwick House*, p. 71. The estate remained unsold.
12. Mary Theresa Odell, *The Old Theatre, Worthing* (Geo. W. Jones, 1938), pp. 19–20.

13. Robert Huish, *Memoirs of Her Late Royal Highness Charlotte Augusta, Princess of Wales* (Thomas Kelly, 1818), quoted in Smail, *Warwick House*, p. 33.

14. Odell, *The Old Theatre, Worthing*, p. 22.

15. National Archives, Add Mss 46189 & 46190, 5 January 1810.

16. List of Electors for the Election of the West Sussex Knight of the Shire (1820).

17. Sarah Ogle's affidavit of 15 April 1834 (National Archives, Add Mss 46130) states that James William Ogle of Beckenham was the eldest of her nine children; and the Deed Poll of Declaration of 1 October 1825 (Add Mss 46192) says that James William Ogle was 'eldest son and heir of the said James Ogle decd.'.

18. *Worthing Gazette*, 8 August 1894.

Chapter 2: Edward Ogle – The Inspiration for 'Mr Parker'

1. Wills of Edward Ogle, National Archives, PROB 11/1616 (drawn up 1809) and of Elizabeth Langstaff, Edward Ogle's mother's sister (drawn up 1793), PROB 11/1240. The latter document refers to land to be shared among various nephews and nieces, including 'James and Edward Ogle' – but then later specifies as executors 'my said nephews, George and Edward Ogle'. This George is not mentioned in Edward's will, or in any other records. From the context it seems likely that Elizabeth Langstaff was referring again to James, and that George was his second name, which was sometimes used to avoid confusion with his father (also James). There is no other evidence for a third Ogle brother.

2. Affidavit of George Ogle (James Ogle's youngest son) of Great Winchester Street, London, dated 19 February 1835, with attached abstract, dated 30 January 1835, from the Rothbury parish register, National Archives, Add Mss 46138. The abstract has added credibility from the fact that it gives the page numbers in the parish register for the respective entries – page 92 for James's baptism in 1757 and page 99 for Edward's in 1759.

3. Deed Poll of Declaration by Sarah Ogle, National Archives, Add Mss 46192, 1 October 1825.

4. www.archive.org/stream/churchheraldryno3farrgoog/churchheraldryno3farrgoog_djvu.txt

5. Ramsay, W. R. H. & Ramsay E. G., 'A Classification of Bow Porcelain from First Patent to Closure: c.1743–1774', *Proceedings of the Royal Society of Victoria* 119, 1 (2007), p. 30.

6. 'The said Edward Ogle left no child.' Affidavit of George Ogle, National Archives, Add Mss 46138.

7. Affidavit of Sarah Ogle, National Archives, Add Mss 46130, 15 April 1834.

8. www.british-history.ac.uk, 63286.

9. National Archives, MJ/SP/1795/SEPT/B/021-029, 24 July 1795 & MS 11936/427/740317, 16 November 1802.

10. www.oldbaileyonline.org, ref. no. 18010415-74.

11. www.oldbaileyonline.org, ref. no. 18010218-81.

12. *The European Magazine and London Review*, Vol. 55 (January–June 1809).

13. Daniel Preston, ed., *Comprehensive Catalogue of the Correspondence and Papers of James Monroe*, Vol. 1 (Greenwood Press, 2000), pp. 176, 186 & 188.

14. *Cobbett's Annual Register* (Cox and Baylis, 1802), Vol. 2, pp. 943–4.

15. According to Henfrey Smail, *Warwick House* (Aldridge Bros, 1952), p. 19, this 'WEBB-footed' mastiff was not a real dog, but represented an old man called Webb who lived in the Steyne. The capitalisation and spelling of 'Webb' is supportive of this. Perhaps Benjamin Bagpipe conflated the dog and the man.

16. John Snewin was the father of Edward Snewin, whose memories of early Worthing form the basis of *Glimpses of Old Worthing* (Aldridge Bros, 1945).

17. Affidavit of George Ogle, National Archives, Add Mss 46138.

18. Edward Ogle's will, National Archives, PROB 11/1616.

19. www.archive.org/stream/churchheraldryno3farrgoog/churchheraldryno3farrgoog_djvu.txt

20. John Shearsmith, *A Topographical Description of Worthing* (G. Verrall, 1824), p. 15.

Chapter 3: Jane Austen's Visit to Worthing

1. The information about Jane Austen's life at the start of this chapter is derived mainly from Park Honan, *Jane Austen: Her Life* (Weidenfeld & Nicolson, 1987) and Clare Tomalin, *Jane Austen: A Life* (Viking, 1997).

2. Deirdre Le Faye, ed., *Jane Austen's Letters*, 4th Edition (Oxford University Press, 2011), p. 112.

3. Deirdre Le Faye, *Chronology of Jane Austen and her Family* (Cambridge University Press, 2006), p. 317.

4. Le Faye, *Jane Austen's Letters*, pp. 116–117.

5. Letter from Fanny Austen to Miss Chapman, 28 July 1805, Kent History and Library Centre, Maidstone.

6. Le Faye, *Jane Austen's Letters*, p. 118.

7. Letter from Fanny Austen to Miss Chapman, 15 September 1805, Kent History and Library Centre.

8. Extracts from the diaries of Fanny Austen, 17–23 December 1805, Kent History and Library Centre.

9. Le Faye, *Chronology*, p. 322.

10. John Mackoull, *A Sketch of Worthing* (J. Mackoull, 1813), pp. 37–8.

11. Le Faye, *Chronology*, p. 324.

Chapter 4: Worthing in 1805

1. A. M. Rowland and T. P. Hudson, *The Victoria History of the County of Sussex*, Vol. 6, Part 1 (1980), p. 96.

2. John Docwra Parry, *An Historical and Descriptive Account of the Coast of Sussex* (Wright & Son, 1833), p. 355.

3. Parry, *An Historical and Descriptive Account*, p. 355.

4. Edward Snewin & Henfrey Smail, *Glimpses of Old Worthing* (Aldridge Bros, 1945), pp. 30–1.

5. *The Universal British Directory of Trade, Commerce and Manufacture* (1798), Vol. 4, p. 580. This directory lists just fourteen 'principal inhabitants' of Worthing. Apart from the brick-maker, the carpenter and the two shopkeepers, all the others are described as 'yeomen'.

6. Henfrey Smail, *Warwick House* (Aldridge Bros, 1952), p. 13.

7. G., *A Tour to Worthing / Or Idle Hours not Idly Spent / Containing a Slight Sketch of the Country, Anecdotes, etc.*, 2nd edition (A. Topping, 1806), p. 30.

8. Parry, *An Historical and Descriptive Account*, p. 353.

9. Henfrey Smail, *The Worthing Map Story* (Aldridge Bros, 1949), p. 71.

10. John Evans, *A Picture of Worthing* (C. Stower, 1805), pp. 30–1.

11. Smail, *The Worthing Map Story*, p. 87.

12. A. J. Waterfield, 'Worthing's Old Buildings', p. 59, in F. W. H. Migeod, *Worthing: A Survey of Times Past and Present* (1938).

13. Snewin & Smail, *Glimpses of Old Worthing*, p. 56.

14. *Post Office Directory of the Six Home Counties* (W. Kelly & Co., 1851), p. 829; *Kelly's Directory 1866*, p. 2150.

15. Snewin & Smail, *Glimpses of Old Worthing*, pp. 127 & 130.

16. Smail, *The Worthing Map Story*, p. 67; Smail, *Warwick House*, p. 15.

17. Ronald Kerridge & Michael Standing, *Worthing: From Saxon Settlement to Seaside Town* (Optimus, 2000), pp. 85 & 89–90.

18. John Nixon's 1808 watercolour of Worthing beach, reproduced on page 57, does not show the building that comprised Stafford's Marine Library and Rebecca House (although the Steyne Hotel, built in 1807, is present), but the 1810 engravings on page 48 do. This suggests that the building was built about 1809. The evidence that Stafford's Library was originally located in Marine Place can be found on p. 88 of Smail, *The Worthing Map Story*. On p. 15 of the 1805 edition of *A Picture of Worthing* John Evans says that the 'Marine Library' run by Mr Stafford is 'situated near the beach', but this description is of course just as applicable to a location in Marine Place as to the library's later home immediately abutting the beach.

19. Parry, *An Historical and Descriptive Account*, pp. 353–4.

20. Rowland and Hudson, *The Victoria History of the County of Sussex*, p. 272. Selden's having been born in a house or cottage on his father's farm at Salvington is not in doubt, only its location.

Chapter 5: Worthing and Sanditon – The Parallels

1. David Selwyn, *Jane Austen and Leisure* (Hambledon Continuum, 1998), p. 57.

2. Jane Austen, *Minor Works* (ed. R. W. Chapman, 1954, revised 1975), p. 368. All extracts from *Sanditon* quoted in this book are taken from this definitive edition of Jane Austen's text, which is faithful to her original manuscript and includes its flaws and idiosyncrasies.

3. Ronald Kerridge & Michael Standing, *Worthing: From Saxon Settlement to Seaside Town* (Optimus, 2000), p. 29.

4. G., *A Tour to Worthing / Or Idle Hours not Idly Spent / Containing a Slight Sketch of the Country, Anecdotes, etc.*, 2nd edition (A. Topping, 1806), p. 30.

5. Edward Snewin & Henfrey Smail, *Glimpses of Old Worthing* (Aldridge Bros, 1945), p. 130.

6. John Shearsmith, *A Topographical Description of Worthing* (G. Verrall, 1824), p. 6.

7. John Evans, *A Picture of Worthing* (C. Stower, 1805), p. 17.

8. Shearsmith, *A Topographical Description*, p. 27; John Docwra Parry, *An Historical and Descriptive Account of the Coast of Sussex* (Wright & Son, 1833), pp. 354 & 356.

9. John Mackoull, *A Sketch of Worthing* (J. Mackoull, 1813), p. 60. All quotations from Mackoull in this chapter are from this 1813 edition of his book.

10. Mackoull, *A Sketch of Worthing*, p. 29. The lines of verse are from *The Seasons* by James Thomson.

Chapter 6: Edward Ogle and the Development of Worthing

1. 'Morrah' and 'Wicks' are the correct spellings. On p. 19 of *A Picture of Worthing* (C. Stower, 1805) John Evans mis-spells both names ('Morah' and 'Wickes').

2. Unless a different source is given, all information about the theatre in this chapter comes from Mary Theresa Odell, *The Old Theatre, Worthing: 1807–1855* (1938). *Of Age Tomorrow* was by Thomas Dibdin (1771–1841) and *The Honey Moon* by John Tobin (1770–1804). Odell has the play as '*The Honeymoon*', while playbills of 25 July 1816 and 13 September 1822 (on which date Horace Smith saw the play, see page 111) have '*Honey Moon*'.

3. Odell, *The Old Theatre, Worthing*, pp. 12–13; Ronald Kerridge & Michael Standing, *Worthing: From Saxon Settlement to Seaside Town* (Optimus, 2000), pp. 98–9.

4. Mary Theresa Odell, *More About the Old Theatre, Worthing* (Aldridge Bros, 1945), p. 48.

5. John Docwra Parry, *An Historical and Descriptive Account of the Coast of Sussex* (Wright & Son, 1833), p. 354.

6. Henfrey Smail, *Warwick House* (Aldridge Bros, 1952), p. 7.

7. In the section on Brighton's Steyne in John Feltham, *A Guide to All the Watering and Sea-Bathing Places* (Longman, Hurst, Rees, Orme & Brown, 1813), pp. 85–6, the spelling 'Steyne' is used throughout.

8. Henfrey Smail, *The Worthing Map Story* (Aldridge Bros, 1949), p. 85; Edward Snewin & Henfrey Smail, *Glimpses of Old Worthing* (Aldridge Bros, 1945), p. 114.

9. Mackoull does not give a first name for his Mr Parsons, but according to Henfrey Smail the Parsons who was manager of the Sea House Hotel in 1813 – and therefore of the Steyne Hotel in 1817, since Mackoull makes clear that his Mr Parsons moved there from the Sea House – was Joseph Parsons. A later owner of the Sea House, from some time after 1826, was George Parsons, and Smail says that he moved there from the Steyne Hotel. If so, the Steyne Hotel must have been managed between *c.* 1817 and *c.* 1827 first by Joseph Parsons and then by George Parsons; who were presumably related. See Smail & Snewin, *Glimpses of Old Worthing*, pp. 58 & 61.

10. Kerridge & Standing, *Worthing*, p. 103.

11. Kerridge & Standing, *Worthing*, p. 108.

12. Snewin & Smail, *Glimpses of Old Worthing*, p. 43; Smail, *The Worthing Map Story*, p. 73.

13. A. M. Rowland and T. P. Hudson, *The Victoria History of the County of Sussex*, Vol. 6, Part 1 (1980), p. 114. The market was authorised by the Worthing Town and Market Act (1809).

14. Kerridge & Standing, *Worthing*, p. 110.

15. Smail, *The Worthing Map Story*, p. 87.

16. Paul Potion, *A Poetical Picture of Worthing and Its Vicinity* (W. Phillips, 1814), p. 33.

Chapter 7: The Life and Grievances of John Mackoull

1. *Historical Research*, Vol. 24, Issue 70 (November 1951), pp. 191–6.

2. *The Herald* (Scotland), 18 November 1992; Major Arthur Griffiths, *Mysteries of Police and Crime: A General Survey of Wrongdoing and Its Pursuit* (1898), Vol. 1, pp. 338–48; Robert Chambers, *Traditions of Edinburgh* (1869 revision of original 1823 edition), pp. 301–4.

3. Mary Theresa Odell, *More About the Old Theatre, Worthing* (Aldridge Bros, 1945), p. 180.

4. The text had already undergone a major revision at the hands of a minor playwright called Thomas Egerton Wilks, who after Grimaldi's death had significantly reduced the original over-long manuscript and also included new material based on his own conversations with Grimaldi.

5. *Memoirs of Joseph Grimaldi*, edited by Boz (2 vols, 1838), Vol. 1, pp. 186–198 & 224–230; Vol. 2, pp. 1–9 & 12–25.

6. Michael Kelly (1762–1826) was an Irish singer and composer with an international reputation.

7. In Mackoull's account of the matter the robber is identified as Treble. The name Jones may have been an alias.

8. A zany was a buffoonish character in old comedies who makes feeble attempts to mimic the clown – cf. Malvolio's comment, 'I protest I take these wise men that crow so at these set kind of fools no better than the fools' zanies.' (Shakespeare, *Twelfth Night*, I, v)

9. John Mackoull, *Abuses of Justice*, 2nd edition (W. Burton, 1812), pp. iv–v.

10. Mackoull, *Abuses of Justice*, pp. 149, 156 & 238.

11. Samuel Butler (1612–80), not as well-known today as his contemporary John Milton (1608–74), was a Royalist poet whose most famous work was 'Hudibras', a long satirical poem attacking Puritanism.

12. Andrew Knapp and William Lee Baldwin, *The Newgate Calendar*, Vol. 4 (J. Robins & Co, 1828), p. 282, cited in John McGowan, *A Tale of Two Cities: Concerning the Robbery in July 1811 of the Paisley Union Bank at Glasgow* (Turlough, 2011).

Chapter 8: Seven Notable Visitors

1. B. C. Southam, *Jane Austen's Literary Manuscripts: A Study of the Novelist's Development through the Surviving Papers* (Oxford University Press, 1964), pp. 105–6.

2. Simon J. White, Robert Bloomfield, *Romanticism and the Poetry of Community* (Ashgate, 2007), pp 67–8.

3. John Evans, *A Picture of Worthing* (C. Stower, 1805), p. 35.

4. Ronald Kerridge & Michael Standing, *Worthing: From Saxon Settlement to Seaside Town* (Optimus, 2000), p. 84.

5. Benson Earle Hill, *Playing About; or, Theatrical Anecdotes and Adventures* (W. Sams, 1840), pp. 15–16.

6. Sarah Wootton, 'The Byronic in Jane Austen's *Persuasion* and *Pride and Prejudice*', *Modern Language Review*, 102 (2007), pp. 26–39.

7. The extracts from Byron's letters of 16, 18 and 26 August are taken from Thomas Moore, *Letters and Journals of Lord Byron, with Notices of His Life* (A. and W. Galignani, 1830), pp. 26–7.

8. Extracts from Henry Long's unpublished reminiscences of Byron (held by the Berg Collection, New York Public Library) appear on pp. 115–6 of Leslie A. Marchand, *Byron: A Biography*, Vol. 1 (John Murray, 1957).

9. The information about Shelley's association with the firm of C. & W. Phillips comes from Samuel J. Looker, *Shelley, Trelawny and Henley: A Study of Three Titans* (Aldridge Bros, 1950).

10. Emily W. Sunstein, *Mary Shelley: Romance and Reality*, pp. 274, 369 & 371.

11. Epes Sargent, ed., *The Poetical Works of Horace Smith and James Smith, with Portraits and a Biographical Sketch* (Mason Brothers, 1857), p. xxii.

12. Various, *The Worthing Parade, Number Two* (Aldridge Bros, 1954), p. 14.

13. Horace Smith's narrative was later included in a three-volume edition of his minor works, but then was forgotten. In *The Worthing Parade, Number Two*, pp. 14–15, Henfrey Smail explains how the piece chanced to come into his hands. It is reprinted in full on pp. 17–25 of the same book, from which the extracts quoted here are taken.

14. See Mary Theresa Odell, *Some Playbills of the Old Theatre, Worthing (1807–1855)* (Aldridge Bros, 1955), pp. 105–115 and Mary Theresa Odell, *The Old Theatre, Worthing (1807–1855)* (Geo. W. Jones, 1938), pp. 50–52.

15. *A Cure for the Heartache* was by Thomas Morton (1764–1838). For *Honey Moon* see note 2 for Chapter 6.

16. Except where separately referenced, the information in the section about Colonel Berkeley comes from the following sources: C. E. Oxberry (ed.), *Oxberry's Dramatic Biography and Histrionic Anecdotes*, Vol. 1 (George Virtue, 1825), pp. 33–46; Sabine Baring-Gould, *Devonshire Characters and Strange Events* (John Lane, The Bodley Head, 1908), pp. 21–34; and the *Edinburgh Annual Register for 1824* (Archibald Constable & Co, 1825), Vol. 17, Part 3, pp. 147–162.

17. Information from the entry for Mrs Bunn in the *Oxford Dictionary of National Biography*.

18. Charles Dickens, *Memoirs of Joseph Grimaldi*, Vol. 2 (Richard Bentley, 1838), pp. 93–99.

19. R. Thorne, ed., *The History of Parliament: The House of Commons 1790–1820* (Boydell and Brewer, 1986), p. 194.

20. The dates given for Maria Foote's birth vary, but the June 1798 date is almost certainly correct, since Miss Foote's mother swore on oath that this was the date (*Oxberry's Dramatic Biography and Histrionic Anecdotes*, Vol. 1, p. 34).

21. *The New Monthly Magazine*, 1 March 1821.

22. *Edinburgh Annual Register for 1824*, p. 147.

23. *The Examiner*, 6 August 1825.

24. Odell, *The Old Theatre, Worthing*, pp. 75–6.

25. *The Sydney Gazette and New South Wales Advertiser*, 1 August 1827.

26. The Hon. Grantley F. Berkeley, *My Life and Recollections* (Hurst & Blackett, 1865), Vol. 2, pp. 141 & 185.

27. *The Examiner*, 6 August 1825.

28. *The Examiner*, 13 November & 20 November 1825.

29. *The Examiner*, 20 November 1825.

30. Odell, *The Old Theatre, Worthing*, pp. 87–8; Odell, *Some Playbills of the Old Theatre, Worthing*, p. 178.

Members of Jane Austen's Family Mentioned in the Text

Revd George Austen (1731–1805)
Jane Austen's father, rector of Steventon, Hampshire from 1761 to 1800. The living was given to him by his rich relation Thomas Knight, who later adopted his third son, Edward (see below).

Cassandra Leigh Austen (1739–1827)
Jane Austen's mother. Lived at Chawton Cottage, near Alton, Hampshire from 1809 onwards, with her two daughters and their friend Martha Lloyd (1765–1843), who in 1828 became the second wife of Jane's second-youngest brother, Francis Austen.

Cassandra Austen (1773–1845)
Fifth of the eight children of Revd and Mrs George Austen, and the elder of their two daughters.

Jane Austen (1775–1817)
Seventh of the eight children of Revd and Mrs George Austen, and the younger of their two daughters.

...

Revd James Austen (1765–1819)
Eldest child of Revd and Mrs George Austen. Became rector of Steventon after his father retired in December 1800. Spent a week in Worthing in October 1817 with his wife and son, and his sister Cassandra (see page 7).

Mary Austen (1771–1843)
Second wife of Revd James Austen, and sister of Martha Lloyd.

Revd James Edward Austen / Austen-Leigh (1798–1874)
Elder of the two children of Revd James Austen and his second wife, Mary. Known in the family as Edward. Recipient of the famous letter from Jane about her little bit of ivory (see page 5). Changed his surname in 1837 to Austen–Leigh as a condition of an inheritance. In 1869 published an important early biography of Jane Austen, drawing on family documents and memories.

...

Edward Austen / Knight (1767–1852)
Third child of Revd and Mrs George Austen. Adopted c. 1783 by his childless distant relations Thomas and Catherine Knight. Inherited the Knight estates at Godmersham, Steventon and Chawton. Took the name of Knight on the death of Catherine Knight in 1812, this being a condition of his inheritance. Lived mainly at Godmersham Park in Kent, but was sometimes at Chawton House with his family, usually in the summer. Travelled to Worthing in September 1805 with his wife, his daughter Fanny, and his sisters Jane and Cassandra.

Elizabeth Austen (1773–1808)
Daughter of Sir Brook and Lady (Fanny) Bridges (1747–1825) of Goodnestone Park in Kent,

sixteen miles from Godmersham. Wife of Edward Austen. Was never Elizabeth Knight, because she died four years before her husband changed his surname to Knight.

Fanny Austen / Knight / Knatchbull (1793–1882)
Eldest of the eleven children of Edward and Elizabeth Austen. Brought up at Godmersham Park. Became Fanny Knight in 1812, a change of name that was initially unwelcome to her. (She wrote in her diary: 'How I hate it!!!!!!') One of Jane Austen's two favourite nieces. Kept a diary all her life, an invaluable source of information about Jane Austen. Married Sir Edward Knatchbull in 1820.

Edward Austen / Knight (1794–1879)
Second eldest of the eleven children of Edward and Elizabeth Austen. Eloped to Gretna Green in 1826 with Mary Dorothea (c.1807–38), one of Sir Edward Knatchbull's daughters by his first marriage, to the intense disapproval of the two fathers and of Fanny, who was not only Edward's sister but also the girl's stepmother.

Fanny Austen

Since it is to Fanny Austen's letters and diaries that we owe our knowledge of Jane Austen's stay in Worthing, it is relevant to include a brief note about Fanny, and about the legacy of her relationship with her aunt, to whom she had been very close.

Fanny's mother died when she was fifteen, and, since she was the eldest child of the family, she came early to adult responsibility, serving in effect as the female head of her widowed father's household. Then, in 1820, at the age of about twenty-seven, and three years after Jane Austen's death, Fanny became the second wife of Sir Edward Knatchbull, a landowner and politician twelve years older than her. He already had six children, and had a further nine with Fanny.

During Cassandra's and Jane's visits to Godmersham, Fanny's mother's attitude to her husband's poor relations had often been slightly patronising, and in old age Fanny herself became increasingly snobbish. Fanny's snobbery coloured Fanny's view of her aunts as the years passed, and in 1869 Fanny wrote a notorious letter to her sister Marianne, who had asked her if she wished to contribute anything to the book about Jane Austen that their cousin James Austen-Leigh was writing.

In her letter Fanny writes that 'Aunt Jane ... was not so *refined* as she ought to have been from her talent' and, while 'too clever not to put aside all possible signs of "common-ness"', she and Cassandra 'were brought up in the most complete ignorance of the World & its ways (I mean as to fashion &c)'. Fanny says that, had her father's marriage not 'brought them into Kent' and the orbit of her father's adoptive mother, Catherine Knight, Cassandra and Jane 'would have been ... very much below par as to good Society & its ways'.

Fanny would not have written in these terms if she had known that her letter would fall into the hands of posterity. Nor, indeed, do the views that she expressed many years afterwards invalidate the closeness of her friendship with her aunt while she was alive. But sadly what has been said cannot be unsaid, and these comments form a sad postscript to one of Jane Austen's closest relationships.

Index of Locations and Buildings in and around Worthing

(Page numbers in bold orange type relate to illustrations. Many of the buildings and streets listed here also appear on the 1805 and 1814 maps of Worthing on pages 47 and 74.)